LITERATURE LINKS TO PHONICS

LITERATURE LINKS TO PHONICS

A Balanced Approach

Karen Morrow Durica

1996
Teacher Ideas Press
A Division of
Libraries Unlimited, Inc.
Englewood, Colorado

DEDICATION

With gratitude and admiration to the authors and illustrators of children's literature, who by their talents and imagination motivate children to read. With gratitude and love to my husband Edward and to our children—Edward, Rebecca, and Adam.

TEACHER IDEAS PRESS
A Division of
Libraries Unlimited, Inc.
P.O. Box 6633
Englewood, CO 80155-6633
(800) 237-6124

Production Editor: Kevin W. Perizzolo
Copy Editor: Susan Brown
Proofreader: Susie Sigman
Typesetter: Michael Florman

Library of Congress Cataloging-in-Publication Data

Durica, Karen Morrow.
    Literature links to phonics : a balanced approach / by Karen
Morrow Durica.
        xiv, 149 p. 22x28 cm.
    Includes bibliographical references and index.
    ISBN 1-56308-353-1
    1. Reading--Phonetic method. 2. Children's literature--Study and
teaching. I. Title.
LB1573.3.D87 1996
372.4'145--dc20   95-51963
                                                           CIP

EPIGRAPH

There is no substitute for a teacher who reads children good stories.

from *Becoming a Nation of Readers: The Report of the Commission on Reading*, 1985.

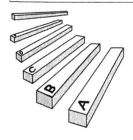

Contents

Preface ix
Introduction xi

Part 1 The Alphabetic Code 1
Chapter 1: The Alphabet 3
  The Consonants 3
  The Vowels 4
    Writing/Spelling Connection 4
    Bibliographic Information and Annotations 4
    Sample Lesson 8
Chapter 2: Common Phonetic Principles 9
  Short Vowel CVC Pattern 10
    Writing/Spelling Connection 10
    Bibliographic Information and Annotations 10
    Sample Lesson 13
  Long Vowel CVVC Pattern 13
    Writing/Spelling Connection 13
    Bibliographic Information and Annotations 13
    Sample Lesson 16
  Long Vowel CVCe Pattern 16
    Writing/Spelling Connection 16
    Bibliographic Information and Annotations 17
    Sample Lesson 20
  Short Vowel VC Pattern 20
    Writing/Spelling Connection 20
    Bibliographic Information and Annotations 21
    Sample Lesson 23
  Long Vowel CV Pattern 24
    Writing/Spelling Connection 24
    Bibliographic Information and Annotations 24
    Sample Lesson 26
  Y as a Vowel 26
    Writing/Spelling Connection 26
    Bibliographic Information and Annotations 26
    Sample Lesson 30
  Consonant Blends 30
    Writing/Spelling Connection 30
    Bibliographic Information and Annotations 31
    Sample Lesson 34

Consonant Digraphs 34
   Writing/Spelling Connection 34
   Bibliographic Information and Annotations 35
   Sample Lesson 43
Final Sound of K 43
   Writing/Spelling Connection 43
   Bibliographic Information and Annotations 44
   Sample Lesson 46
Diphthongs 46
   Writing/Spelling Connection 46
   Bibliographic Information and Annotations 47
   Sample Lesson 50
R-Controlled Vowels 50
   Writing/Spelling Connection 50
   Bibliographic Information and Annotations 51
   Sample Lesson 54
Soft and Hard G and C 54
   Writing/Spelling Connection 54
   Bibliographic Information and Annotations 55
   Sample Lesson 58
Word Ending—ing 58
   Writing/Spelling Connection 58
   Bibliographic Information and Annotations 59
   Sample Lesson 62
Word Ending—ed 62
   Writing/Spelling Connection 62
   Bibliographic Information and Annotations 63
   Sample Lesson 66
Part 2 High-Frequency Words 67
Chapter 3: Core Words 69
   Alphabetical List with Bibliographies 71
Chapter 4: Common Concepts 111
   Alphabetical List with Bibliographies 111

Appendix A: Phonics Generalizations 117
Appendix B: High-Frequency Words in Order of Frequency 119
Appendix C: High-Frequency Words in Alphabetical Order 121
Appendix D: Basic Sight Vocabulary 123
Appendix E: Publishers' Addresses 125
References 127
Suggestions for Further Reading 129
Index 131
About the Author 150

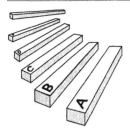

Preface

Nothing is more central to the concept of education than literacy. The ability of students to read and write is of paramount concern to educators and parents. Students who struggle with reading are marked as possibly learning disabled as early as first grade. Literacy is so crucial to our success in society that Don Holdaway states in his book, *The Foundations of Literacy*: "If we continue to make literacy a criterion for basic dignity in our society, we cannot tolerate the failure with its poignantly modern forms of misery and maladjustment. . . . [W]e should either find a *preventive* solution or excuse a large proportion of children from school attendance" (Holdaway 1979, 12).

Great emphasis is currently placed on the concept of early intervention. Clay stresses that children, whatever their level of maturity, will be learning *something* as they are exposed to instruction at school. Without early intervention, they will have many opportunities to practice inappropriate reading behaviors, and their growing misconceptions about print will further complicate their progress (Clay 1985). Delayed progress in reading, especially after the second grade, triggers problems with self-esteem and general feelings of incompetency. "When a child cannot read the problem goes beyond reading to include many other school problems. The major goal for these early intervention efforts is to help children before reading failure becomes failure in all areas of the curriculum and the gap is too great to be repaired" (Pinnell in Allen and Mason 1989, 181).

In addition to their concern about early intervention, educators are discussing what is indeed the best way to teach these emerging and beginning readers. Chall discusses in "The Great Debate" (1983) whether the emphasis in reading instruction should rest with exposure to print and strategic use of contextual clues or with the direct instruction and use of decoding skills and word analysis. Recent research on phonemic awareness suggests that students' abilities to perform various phonemic tasks are "the best predictors of the ease of early reading acquisition—better than anything else that we know of, including IQ" (Stanovich 1994, 284). Yet Kenneth Goodman, during a conference highlighting his book *Phonics Phacts*, stressed that children have phonemic awareness if they are able to speak, and its relationship to reading ability is of little importance (CCIRA Conference, Denver, Colorado, February 4, 1994). Although phonemic awareness differs from knowledge of phonics generalizations, this research adds to the argument of the place of phonics and phonemic training in reading instruction.

The pendulum swings from one end to the other, and educators wait for those rational, productive eras when its arc spans the middle, when the best of all worlds is used to help bring students to their full potential as literate human beings. In twenty-five years of teaching, I have used everything from high-frequency word flashcards and phonics worksheets to Big Books and literature logs. My experiences have taught me that there is some value in everything, and that no one method is "the only way." Indeed, the best approach has been a balanced approach.

This book is intended to be a resource for teachers who recognize both the importance of direct skills instruction in reading and the value of presenting that instruction in the context of authentic literature. The books listed in this resource are ones commonly found in primary classrooms and ones that the author has used successfully with students. They are stories most children enjoy, and they have numerous characteristics that make them worthwhile literature for emergent, beginning, and independent readers. They represent various themes and include both fiction and nonfiction selections. These books contain common phonetic elements or repeated high-frequency words and therefore can be used as a source for direct instruction in those areas. In no way are they the *only* books that can be used to present basic phonetic elements or high-frequency words, nor is the phonics principle or high-frequency word under which a book is listed the only one that can be found in that book. Hopefully, teachers will add to the lists presented in this book as they find literature they enjoy sharing with their students. These books do offer a starting point for teachers whose students need instruction and practice in using the graphophonic system of the English language and in building their sight-word vocabulary.

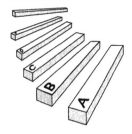

Introduction

What Is Reading?

Some people continue to look at reading as an accumulation of subskills that when put together result in word recognition and comprehension. However, most educators accept the research that supports reading as a complex problem-solving process involving prior knowledge, purpose of reading, prediction, confirmation, and integration (Clay 1991; DeFord, Lyons, and Pinnell 1991; Smith 1983a, 1982b; Routman 1991a, 1988b). The following figure illustrates a simplified version of the process used by fluent readers as they approach print.

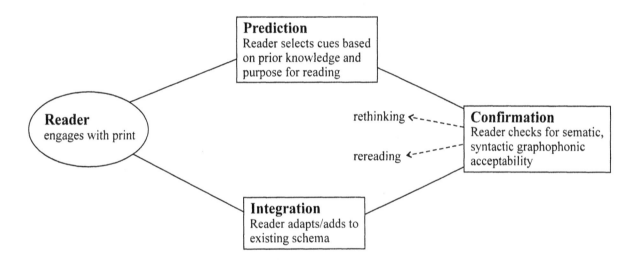

What Are the Three Cueing Systems?

Fluent readers interact with text by immediately engaging what they already know about the topic and by using what they understand about printed language. They begin to make predictions based on this prior knowledge and read to confirm those predictions. Fluent readers confirm their predictions by using all three cueing systems simultaneously and rapidly. They check for semantic acceptability, or "Does it make sense?"; they check for syntactic acceptability, or "Is that how language sounds?"; and they check for graphophonic acceptability, or "Is that how I would expect that word to look? Are those the letters I would expect to find in that word?" Fluent readers use these strategies flexibly and orchestrate them to meet the degree of complexity in the reading material (Clay 1991, 3).

Successful readers establish a cross-checking system by using these three cueing systems. If their prediction is confirmed, they continue to read. If one or more of the cueing systems signals that there is an error, fluent readers will either rethink their prediction or reread the passage in hopes of picking up additional clues to help them find the meaning of the text. Once readers confirm their predictions, they integrate the ideas about the topic and the refined strategies or skills used to arrive at confirmation into their existing schema. Thus they modify, alter, or embellish the knowledge they will incorporate into their next prediction and subsequent readings. Fluent readers develop this self-extending system, which enables them to improve their reading ability each time they read, independent of instruction (DeFord, Lyons, and Pinnell 1991, 97, 104).

All three cueing systems are valuable and help students read successfully. Readers cannot depend on one system alone. To understand this more clearly, look at the following sentence:

The farmer is walking in the field.

Readers concerned only with semantics may read the word *father* for *farmer* because they are predicting that the male figure presented is a father of a family. That assumption may not make a difference in some stories; in others, a mystery perhaps, it may be a significant error. Readers relying only on syntactic cues may read the word *is* as *isn't*, which still sounds like acceptable language, but, of course, changes the meaning of the text. Readers depending solely on graphophonic acceptability may read something like "The farmer is standing in the felt." (This mistake actually occurred with a student of mine!) *Felt* and *field* are close enough visually to satisfy some readers. Without using language structure and meaning to cross-check for comprehension, a student could possibly (and did!) go right on reading. Therefore, teachers concerned about providing the best foundation for progress in literacy should make their students well aware of all three language cues, provide direct instruction in all three areas, model how to use these systems to arrive at the meaning of the text, and allow ample time for students to practice using these strategies and skills in the reading of authentic literature.

What Is the Place of Phonics Instruction?

As mentioned above, the graphophonic cueing system is one of the three systems that fluent readers use to derive the meaning from a text. Using this system alone or as the main way to achieve word accuracy and comprehension is inefficient and ineffective. As Frank Smith pointed out in *Essays into Literacy*: "166 rules would be required to account for the most frequent correspondences in just 6000 one- and two-syllable words in the vocabulary of six to nine year olds—and these 166 rules would still not account for over 10 percent of the most common words which would have to be excluded as 'exceptions'" (Smith 1983).

However, is it important that students learn the relationships between letters and sounds? Of course! Is it important that students have access to an immediate way to distinguish between *cap* and *cape?* Of course! Are there some basic phonetic elements reliable enough to make them worth learning? I believe there are.

Is it equally important for students to build a strong base of words they recognize immediately? Yes. "Skilled readers tend to use as little visual knowledge as possible, scanning for just enough information to check on the meaning" (Clay 1991, 235). Sight recognition of the common words that hold text together allows students to move through text more easily and offers a basis for monitoring accuracy. Students who must labor through too many words lose not only the fluency of proficient oral reading, but also sacrifice the flow of ideas necessary to maintain comprehension. A basic sight vocabulary enables students to employ the other strategies of the cueing systems. "Skilled readers sample [text] effectively because they know a great number of words at sight and the phrases and patterns they frequently occur in" (*Reading in Junior Classes* 1994).

The problem with isolated instruction in either phonics or high-frequency words occurs when teachers try to separate those elements from their function within the process of reading itself. I have taught children who believe reading is "saying the right words in the right order." They can perform all kinds of linguistic "gymnastics," pronounce even the most complicated multisyllabic words, yet neither enjoy their feat nor comprehend the message behind the sentence through which they have just struggled.

This resource provides lists of literature that can be used to increase students' awareness of reliable phonetic elements and to increase their sight-word vocabulary. Part 1 enables the teacher to direct the students' attention to phonetic elements within a given book and to help reinforce the relationship between knowledge of phonics and its value in the process of reading. Emphasis should be given to the importance of including the other two cueing systems to cross-check for accuracy.

Each of the main phonetic principles is covered in a separate section. Each section includes a Writing/Spelling Connection because the need to apply phonetic principles is evident more often in writing than in reading. Readers have many clues to consider when reading an unknown word, but when writers are trying to convey a message, they must know which letter represents which sound. Andrea Butler states that we learn "phonics through writing for reading" (Butler 1994). An annotated bibliography follows the Writing/Spelling Connection, and the final component of each phonetic section is a sample lesson that includes a follow-up activity most children can do independently. Follow-up activities are meant to be fun and provide opportunities for children to "play with words." As Donald Graves states when discussing young children's literacy efforts, "the tone should be one of discovery" (Graves 1994, 198).

Part 2 lists high-frequency words and books in which they appear. Repeated exposure to these words increases the speed with which students are able to recognize them and provides varied situations in which the words can be found, thus stretching the flexibility of sight-word application. Building a sight vocabulary contributes to both reading and writing. "By the time the list of core words a child controls grows to about 40, the writer controls most of the letter/sound associations of the language, plus the most frequent and regular spelling correspondences"(Clay 1991, 244). This section includes books for both core words and for concepts, such as color words or punctuation.

How Should This Book Be Used?

You should choose a book to read with students primarily because the book is worthwhile: worthwhile because it can teach them something new about themselves or their world; worthwhile because it can introduce them to a new concept of printed language; worthwhile because it is just a fun story to read. Whatever your reason for choosing a text, make sure the book is one you and your students will enjoy exploring together. Perhaps the greatest change I have observed in literacy instruction over the past twenty-five years is the increase in the *enjoyment* of reading. Don't deprive your students of enjoying books by selecting a piece you feel you must drudge through so they can encounter this particular skill. "[S]tories have more value than letter lessons" (Clay 1991, 29). There is enough wonderful literature out today that your first objective can be to enjoy the story. We accomplish nothing if we produce students who are capable of reading but choose not to do so because the books to which they have been exposed contained boring, lifeless stories. The skills and strategies we teach our children are of no importance if they will not use them to enhance their lives long after they leave us. Mark Twain is credited with saying that the man who does not read good books has no advantage over the man who cannot read them.

Provide ample time for your students to explore reading and writing. Direct instruction is necessary, but don't deprive your students of time to use what they are learning about print by engaging in authentic reading and writing. The key is a balanced approach. The best phonics instruction comes out of the need to solve a real reading or writing problem. Children should never be deprived of a reading experience or a writing activity because they do not know a rule. Show them instead how applying graphophonic knowledge can help them successfully read or write the message. Monitor your lessons so that the majority of reading or writing time is spent doing just that—reading and writing!

Based on the above concepts, the recommendations for using this resource are as follows:

1. Choose a book because it has a story you want to share with the students. Levels of difficulty are suggested should you intend the students to read the books themselves. **A** indicates books appropriate for an emergent reader; **B**, a beginning reader; **C**, a more independent reader. Of course, all the books make great read-alouds.

2. Read the book and enjoy the ideas, characters, plot, or other literary features.

3. Choose selected words, phrases, or sentences from the text that contain the phonetic element on which you wish to focus or the high-frequency word you wish to emphasize.

4. For a phonetic element, ask the children if they notice any commonalities among the words or in the sentences or phrases.

5. For a high-frequency word, ask the children to see how many times they can find the word in the text or elsewhere in the room (signs, charts)—go on a "word hunt."

6. After discussion, begin direct instruction of the phonetic principle or high-frequency word. (Sample lessons or activities are included under each phonetic element and in the introduction to Part 2.)

7. Return to the text and discuss other ways students may know what those words are (picture clues, meaning clues, grammar clues); emphasize the idea of cross-checking by using the *three* cueing systems.

8. Whenever possible, demonstrate how the phonetic principle or high-frequency word is used in writing because this strengthens its foundation as a part of printed language and builds on the relationship between reading and writing.

9. Implement suggested follow-up activities for additional practice, as indicated by your students' needs and interests. Keep these *fun*; **don't make them drills.**

10. Use other books listed in the same section to reinforce or review the knowledge and skill of a particular lesson only if the book has value above and beyond the phonics or high-frequency word component.

This book does not recommend compromising the integrity of a story for the sake of presenting a phonics or high-frequency word lesson.

PART 1
THE ALPHABETIC CODE

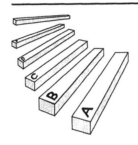

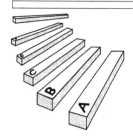

Chapter 1

The Alphabet

Identifying the letters of the alphabet and the sounds associated with them has been a major goal of preschools, kindergartens, and first grades across the nation for many years. That "direct instruction of alphabetic coding facilitates early reading acquisition is one of the most well established conclusions in all behavioral science" (Stanovich 1994, 286). Twenty-five years of teaching experience has supported the observation that students entering first grade with solid letter identification skills have a distinct advantage over those children who have made little or no associations regarding alphabetic symbols.

The increasing body of research regarding phonemic awareness further supports the concept of the importance of being able to hear and distinguish between the individual phonemes that comprise speech. Adams proposes that phonemic awareness may be the "most important core and causal factor separating normal and disabled readers" (1990, 305). Certainly when knowledge of the visual and auditory aspects of the alphabet is consistent and spontaneous, students are free to use the alphabetic code as a tool to help them pursue the more intricate concepts of print and meaning that are involved in reading.

Alphabet books are more numerous than any other genre of children's literature. They range from the simple format of a single picture matched to a letter to more elaborate presentations of stories or rhymes built around each letter, to the entire alphabet book presenting a single theme. The bibliography that follows the explanation of consonants and vowels contains both alphabet books in the pure definition of the word and books that emphasize phonemes, or the sounds of our language, but not necessarily following an alphabet sequence. The former books are best for directing attention to letter recognition and isolated sound; the latter books are beneficial for increasing phonemic awareness. Books marked with an asterisk (*) indicate literature particularly recommended for increasing phonemic awareness because of the alliteration or rhyme they contain. Levels of difficulty are not listed in this bibliography because most of the selections are intended to be read with or to the students.

The Consonants

In English articulation, consonants are distinguished from vowels as speech sounds produced by occluding, diverting, or obstructing the flow of air. A more practical explanation for young learners is that the consonants more consistently make one sound, whereas the vowels have both a long and a short sound. Experience has shown that consonant sounds, particularly those whose sounds cannot be sustained (for example, *b* versus *s*) are best taught within the context of a word. In other words, learning "*b—bus*" is preferable to "*b—ba*." Children tend to add sounds to the consonant when they must pronounce what I call "stopper" consonants in isolation. This habit can cause confusion when they begin to write words using the consonant sounds they know.

An activity I find particularly helpful with emphasizing consonant sounds is "I'm going to _____". If the consonant being studied is *B*, we might go to **B**oston. To get on the train each student must say a word that begins with *B*. To make the game more challenging for advanced learners, each child must supply a word, plus repeat the words given previously. For example, "I'm going to Boston and I'm bringing a *blanket* (student's choice) and a *banana, basketball, baby, balloon* and a *bear* (choices made by the first five students). The number of students in a group can be varied to meet the needs of the students. Be sure to show the children where the city, state, or country is; you might even discuss what they think it would be like there.

The Vowels

In contrast to consonants, vowels are letters representing the sounds made without occluding, diverting, or obstructing the flow of air. More simply stated, they are *a, e, i, o, u,* and sometimes *y* and *w*. The five constant vowels have a long and a short sound. The long sound is that sound made by saying the vowel's name: *a* as in *ate*; *e* as in *eel*; *i* as in *ice*; *o* as in *ocean*; and *u* as in *unicorn*. The short sound is that sound made most often by the vowel when it is the only vowel in a word between two consonants: *a* as in *cat*; *e* as in *bell*; *i* as in *him*; *o* as in *sod*; and *u* as in *tub*. The letters *y* and *w* are considered to be vowels only at the end of a word or syllable: *y* as in *my* or *funny*; *w* as in *how* or *snow* (*w* is actually part of a diphthong).

Although the vowels are no more difficult to identify than the consonants, many children find their sounds more difficult to recall and to reproduce in isolation. Short sounds can be particularly confusing. Whenever possible, use the students' names to emphasize vowel sounds. Names are extremely meaningful to children, both their own and those of their friends. Short *a* is not as hard to remember if you associate it with *Allison*, or short *e* with *Ed*. Be sure to list everyone's name beneath the appropriate letter of the alphabet; names are a potent, meaningful tool.

Likewise, vowel charts make a greater impression if the words are in some context. Illustrating sentences like the following makes it easier for children to recall the key words they want to associate with particular vowel sounds.

   A—Annie Alligator eats acorns.

   E—Edward Eskimo raises eels.

   I—Isabel Inchworm likes ice cream.

   O—Oliver Octopus lives in the ocean.

   U—Uncle Umbro rides a unicorn.

   Y—Sly Sally has a yellow mask.

   W—Brown Cow likes wild grass.

When possible, have the students compose the sentences for the class; that makes the chart even more meaningful.

An activity I find quite helpful, as well as enjoyable when emphasizing vowels is introducing food that contains a particular vowel sound. Children love to snack, and eating in class is particularly memorable. Do make sure you have checked for allergies so the activity does not become more memorable than you had intended! I have used the following items successfully:

long a: cake	short a: apples
long e: cheese	short e: jello
long i: ice cream	short i: pickles (or licorice)
long o: toast	short o: hot dogs
long u: juice	short u: buns or nuts (watch allergies here)

Writing/Spelling Connection

The most important alphabet book the children will have is the one they write themselves. Each student should have a blank book with one letter, presented in both capital and lower case form, on the top or bottom of each page. Whatever key word means something to the child is placed on that page in his or her book. *Keesha* may not be the word you would pick to remember the sound of *k*, but if that is the name of Sarah's dog, and she knows it begins with a *k*, you can count on that association being a permanent one for her. Class books can be made patterned after alphabet books read aloud. For example, after reading *A Farmer's Alphabet* by Mary Azarian, direct the class in making "A First Grader's Alphabet."

Bibliographic Information and Annotations

*Ahlberg, J., and A. Ahlberg. *Each Peach Pear Plum*. New York: Scholastic, 1978. An "I Spy" format uses rhymes from familiar Mother Goose stories.
Feature: Good book to use as basis for playing "I Spy" to look for objects that begin with the same letter of the alphabet or objects that rhyme.

Aylesworth, J. *Old Black Fly*. New York: Scholastic, 1992. After flying through the alphabet the old black fly meets his demise.
Feature: Good book for prediction; ask students to predict what the fly will fly by next.

Azarian, M. *A Farmer's Alphabet*. Boston: David R. Godine, 1981. Black-and-white prints from woodcuts enhance this rural alphabet.
Feature: Can be used as a basis for a class alphabet book centered on a theme like "a first grader's alphabet" or "a city alphabet."

*Berenstain, S., and J. Berenstain. *The Berenstain's B Book.* New York: Random House, 1971. All words in this text begin with a *b.*
Feature: Can discuss what other *b* words could be added within the context of the story, or can be used as the basis for the children's own story using a different letter.

*Brown, M. W. *Four Fur Feet.* New York: Doubleday, 1993. Repeated pattern of *f* alliteration appears as animal makes its way around the world.
Feature: Book must be turned as animal travels around the world.

*Buller, J., and S. Schade. *I Love You, Good Night.* New York: Simon & Schuster, 1988. A mother and child say good night by telling each other how much one loves the other in delightful rhymes.
Feature: Encourages the readers to make up rhymes of their own.

*Carter, D. *More Bugs in Boxes.* New York: Simon & Schuster, 1990. Questions and answers about imaginative bugs are presented in this colorful pop-up book.
Feature: Good book for discussion of alliteration.

Ehlert, L. *Eating the Alphabet: Fruits and Vegetables from A to Z.* San Diego, Cal.: Harcourt Brace Jovanovich, 1989. Common and less familiar fruits and vegetables are labeled and illustrated.
Feature: Interesting facts about each food item appear in a glossary; good book to integrate with health unit.

*Emberley, B. *Drummer Hoff.* New York: Simon & Schuster, 1967. Each member of the brigade has his job in firing the cannon; strong use of rhyme used to read names.
Feature: Caldecott winner; can be used as a pattern for children to write a job that would rhyme with their own first or last name.

*Gaulke, G. *Where Is My Shoe?* New York: Holt, Rinehart & Winston, 1965. Little girl asks different animals if they have found her missing shoe.
Feature: Can be used to discuss the concept of pairs and develop related vocabulary.

*Gordon, J. *Six Sleepy Sheep.* New York: Puffin Books, 1991. Readers encounter six sheep who are trying to fall asleep by engaging in all kinds of activities using the sound of *s.*
Feature: Strong alliteration can be used as a pattern for others' alliterations or alliterations using a different consonant.

Greenfield, E. *Aaron and Gayla's Alphabet Book.* New York: Black Butterfly Children's Books, 1993. African-American children play through the alphabet; many highlighted words are action words.
Feature: Can be used as a basis for talking about verbs as action words.

*Hague, K. *Alphabears.* New York: Henry Holt, 1984. Teddy bears introduce the alphabet using alliteration containing their names.
Feature: Each student can write and illustrate an alliteration based on his or her name.

*Hall, N. *Snoopy's Book of Opposites.* New York: Golden Books, 1987. Famous Charles M. Schultz characters use rhyme to demonstrate opposites.
Feature: Can be used to study common opposites.

Isadora, R. *City Seen From A to Z.* New York: Greenwillow, 1983. Pictures and the alphabet introduce diversity and characteristics of the city.
Feature: Relate to Azarian's *A Farmer's Alphabet.*

*Jorgensen, G. *Crocodile Beat.* Crystal Lake, Ill.: Rigby, 1988. Rhythmic story of crocodile coming to spoil jungle animals' celebration.
Feature: Tape available; good book for dramatization.

Leonard, M. *Alphabet Bandits.* Mahwah, N.J.: Troll, 1990. Raccoons eat foods from A to Z.
Feature: Relate to Ehlert's book, *Eating the Alphabet: Fruits and Vegetables,* and Shelby's book, *Potluck.*

Martin, B., and J. Archambault. *Chicka-Chicka Boom Boom.* New York: Scholastic, 1989. Rhythmic story of letters racing up and falling down from a coconut tree.
Feature: Both upper and lower case letters are presented; children can go on a letter "hunt" and try to find a given letter on the page.

*Marzollo, J. *I'm Tyrannosaurus.* New York: G. P. Putman's Sons, 1970. Rhyme is used to explain dinosaur names.
Feature: Can be used to introduce the concept of prefixes and suffixes.

Mayer, M. *The Unicorn Alphabet.* New York: Dial, 1989. Stories focus on the mythical unicorn and other beliefs of medieval times.
Feature: Flowers decorate page borders and are defined in a glossary.

McDonald, M. *Debra's Dog*. Crystal Lake, Ill.: Rigby, 1984. Each letter describes an attribute of Debra's dog.

Feature: Can be used as a pattern for a book about a custodian, principal, or some other character known to the students.

Musgrove, M. *Ashanti to Zulu: African Traditions*. New York: Dial, 1976. Researched facts about twenty-six tribes present the culture and language of African people.

Feature: Caldecott winner; provides good basis for multicultural discussion.

Pallotta, J. *The Icky Bug Alphabet Book*. Watertown, Mass.: Charlesbridge, 1986. A bug for each letter of the alphabet is humorously presented and illustrated.

Feature: Pallotta has a series of similar alphabet books that can be used as supplements to science themes.

Reit, S. *Things That Go—A Traveling Alphabet*. New York: Byron Press Visual, 1990. Each letter explains a different mode of transportation.

Feature: Nonfiction; can be used for categorizing: things that fly, crawl, sing.

Rice, J. *Cowboy Alphabet*. Gretna, La.: Pelican, 1990. Ranch life in the southwestern United States is presented using letters of the alphabet.

Feature: Can be used to discuss different occupations or life styles.

*Seuss, T. *Dr. Seuss's ABC*. New York: Random House, 1963. Reading level is advanced, but there are lots of fun words that emphasize each sound.

Feature: Can be used as the pattern for making fun words by maintaining the rime (last part of the word) and changing the onset (initial letter/sound).

*Seuss, T. *Fox in Socks*. New York: Random House, 1965. Popular Seuss tongue-twisters expose readers to lots of language play, including vowel changes.

Feature: Can be used to develop flip charts that change middle vowel to make new word.

Shelby, A. *Potluck*. New York: Orchard Books, 1994. Children bring multiethnic food to a potluck fare; each letter presents a different dish.

Feature: Can be used to help plan a class potluck.

*Slater, T. *Dining with Prunella*. Cleveland, Ohio: Small Package, 1991. Multiple choices are offered to readers who are asked to find rhymes about picky Prunella's eating habits.

Feature: Can be used as a pattern for writing riddles whose answer rhymes with the clue. Example: "I'm small and I squeak and I live in a house. I'm a cat, or a dog or a little gray _____." [mouse]

*Strauss, B., and H. Friedland. *See You Later Alligator*. Los Angeles: Price Stern Sloan, 1987. Humorous book of rhyming word plays.

Feature: Good inspiration for creating own couplets.

Thornhill, J. *The Wildlife ABC*. New York: Half Moon Books, 1994. Centers on theme of wildlife animals; page borders add special interest.

Feature: Includes nature notes with factual information about each animal.

Van Allsburg, C. *The Z Was Zapped*. Boston: Houghton Mifflin, 1987. A play of twenty-six acts presents each letter with descriptions using verbs and nouns.

Feature: Can be used as an introduction to naming words and action words.

Whitehead, P. *Dinosaur Alphabet Book*. Mahwah, N.J.: Troll, 1985. Prehistoric creatures and times are explained by using words that represent each letter of the alphabet.

Feature: Capitalizes on children's natural interest in dinosaurs.

*Wood, A. *Quick as a Cricket*. Singapore. Child's Play (International), 1982. Beautiful illustrations and use of similes help describe a child's personality.

Feature: Good book to use to introduce similes; children can write and illustrate a simile that describes them.

Personal Additions:

Sample Lesson—The Alphabet

Note:

Whenever possible, lessons working with the alphabet should integrate work with both letter identification and the sound or sounds the letter makes.

Books:

Debra's Dog; *Alphabet Bandits*; *The Unicorn Alphabet*; *The Icky Bug Alphabet Book*; *A Farmer's Alphabet*; et al.

Introduction:

"We're going on a "Q hunt today. I'm going to give each group several alphabet books and I'd like you to find what picture or word is on the page for *q*." Allow needed time for group work.

Lesson:

Gather children and ask for various words found for the letter *q*. List words on a chart or board. See if children realize the *q* is followed by a *u*; if not, discuss that characteristic of the letter *q* in the English language.

Ask children if they can think of any other words that begin with the *qu* sound; list them (phonemic awareness activity).

Have children return to their individual alphabet books and choose a key word they want to write or illustrate to help them remember the sound of *qu*. Read "Smart" from Shel Silverstein's *Where the Sidewalk Ends*; ask the children to listen for the *qu* word in the poem (phonemic awareness activity).

Follow-up activity:

Reinforce the *qu* sound by working the words *quickly* or *quietly* onto the daily message board; display a 12-x-18-inch tagboard entitled *Qu* and allow children to add *qu* words they find in their reading (visual awareness) or hear as you read aloud to them (phonemic awareness).

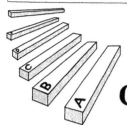

Chapter 2

Common Phonetic Principles

Given a list of English words in isolation it immediately becomes apparent that knowledge of consonant and vowel sounds alone is not enough for successful decoding. How many vowels are in a word, where the vowels and consonants occur, and in what order they are presented makes the difference between saying *pan* or *pain*, *on* or *no*, and *at* or *ate*. The command "sound it out" is not easily followed if students do not have some concept of the basic phonetic patterns common in many English words. "To operate sounding-out behaviors two kinds of analysis must be brought into strict coordination:

an auditory, temporal analysis of the sound sequences in spoken words (hearing sounds in words)

and the visual and spatial analysis from left to right of letters or clusters of letters in a written word" (Clay 1991, 235).

This basic ability to work with the graphophonic cueing system is enhanced by knowledge of common phonetic principles, or phonics generalizations. In spite of exceptions, words fall into phonetic patterns often enough to make some of the more common patterns worth teaching to students. Phonics generalizations can be useful tools, but like all tools, if used improperly, can cause more harm than good.

For example, in my experience as a reading specialist I have worked with students who knew sound/letter relationships and phonics so well that they literally decoded their way across a line of print. They "sounded out" everything, even words that they knew by sight. They did not enjoy reading and retained little of what they read because their focus was correctly decoding each word in a sentence—a tedious task at best. Using the graphophonic cueing system was their only strategy to unlocking the printed message before them. Phonics hurt

more than helped here because the focus of reading was on a word level.

On the other hand, I have also encountered students who knew so little of the graphophonic cueing system that they could not tell me if the word was *mom* or *mother*; they had no immediate way to confirm whether the character in the story got a new *cap* or a new *cape*. Focus was on meaning, but meaning suffered because the readers could not apply their knowledge of the graphophonic cueing system to confirm their predictions; therefore, such strategies as re-reading or reading on could not be used as successfully. Here, the lack of phonics hurt the readers' progress.

Once again, the manner in which phonics is taught and the degree to which it is related to the reading process as a whole will decide its value and usefulness to the students. Phonics must be taught along with authentic reading so students, especially those struggling with literacy, can see its connection to the syntactic and semantic cueing systems and to the problem-solving process that is reading. Children who go through phonics first and in isolation from real reading experiences "see little reason for it; . . . there is little incentive to learn phonics if you rarely read or write" (Butler 1994).

The remainder of this chapter presents phonics generalizations that can be understood and applied by most primary-school children. The bibliography following each principle provides sources containing a repetition of words to which the particular phonetic element can be applied. Keep in mind that studying words in isolation from text is valuable only if those words are eventually brought back to the text. Be sure to model how specific phonics skills can be used with the other two cueing systems to develop a self-monitoring, self-extending approach to reading.

Short Vowel CVC Pattern

When a single vowel comes between two consonants it is usually short.

Examples:

hat	red	milk	box	jump
hand	tent	pig	top	bun
quack*	next	hill	sock	duck

*The *u* in *quack* is kept with the *q* and is not considered a separate vowel.

Writing/Spelling Connection

Students can be taught that every English word has at least one vowel. Later, the knowledge that every syllable has at least one vowel can be added. Students can use this knowledge to increase their writing vocabulary. For example, once students know the word **cat**, they can be shown how substituting initial letters like *h*, *p*, *s*, or *b* can make the words *hat*, *pat*, *sat*, and *bat*.

Bibliographic Information and Annotations

Author	Title	Information	Level
Butler, A.	*Jack-in-the-Box.*	Crystal Lake, Ill.: Rigby, 1989. Colorful boxes open up to reveal a jack-in-the-box.	A
Feature: Reinforces color words; sentence structure begins with the word *in*.			
Cowley, J.	*The Bicycle.*	San Diego, Calif.: Wright Group, 1983. A bicycle holds several circus performers—almost!	A
Feature: Good for short *o* words.			
Cowley, J.	*The Big Hill.*	San Diego, Calif.: Wright Group, 1983. Children enjoy many outdoor activities made possible by the big hill.	A
Feature: Good basis for discussion of action words.			
Cowley, J.	*Dan, the Flying Man.*	San Diego, Calif.: Wright Group, 1983. Everyone runs all over town trying to catch Dan.	A
Feature: Contains directional words; good for short *a* words.			
Cowley, J.	*Dinner!*	San Diego, Calif.: Wright Group, 1986. Mother bird brings worm to baby chick.	A
Feature: Book has directional words; relate to *Rosie's Walk* by Hutchins.			
Cowley, J.	*No, No.*	San Diego, Calif.: Wright Group, 1988. Cyclical format that presents everyone running in circles.	A
Feature: Relate to cyclical theme in Numeroff's *If You Give a Mouse a Cookie*.			
Gregorich, B.	*The Gum on the Drum.*	Grand Haven, Mich.: School Zone, 1984. Bear winds up with a new haircut because he put gum on the drum.	A
Feature: Can be used for a discussion of cause and effect.			
Gregorich, B.	*I Want a Pet.*	New York: School Zone, 1984. Process of elimination results in two green pets.	A
Feature: Discuss using process of elimination in solving some problems requiring decision-making; reinforces color words.			

Author	Title	Information	Level
King, S.	*Baby's Dinner.*	Crystal Lake, Ill.: Rigby, 1989. Baby plays with food until she ends up in the tub.	A
Feature: Use of onomatopoeia, word play.			
Lawrence, L.	*Chew Chew Chew.*	Crystal Lake, Ill.: Rigby, 1989. Goats devour anything and everything.	A
Feature: Use of onomatopoeia.			
Neville, P.	*Going Fishing.*	Crystal Lake, Ill.: Rigby, 1989. Girl and her dog catch dinner.	A
Feature: Good book to use for building word families.			
Van Allen, R.	*I Can Spell Dinosaur.*	New York: DLM Teacher Resource, 1985. Story presents common word families and ends with dinosaur.	A
Feature: Can be used as basis for presenting other short-vowel word families; discuss other words students can spell.			
Borden, L.	*Caps, Hats, Socks and Mittens.*	New York: Scholastic, 1989. Poems express childhood enjoyment of the four seasons.	B
Feature: Relate to other seasonal poems.			
Butler, A.	*Excuses, Excuses.*	Crystal Lake, Ill.: Rigby, 1984. Children have all kinds of excuses for being late, but does the teacher?	B
Feature: Can be used to introduce the format of thought bubbles.			
Cowley, J.	*Wishy Washy Day.*	San Diego, Calif.: Wright Group, 1993. Mrs. Wishy Washy has a mishap while looking for those dirty animals.	B
Feature: Relate to Cowley's *Mrs. Wishy Washy.*			
Crawford, T.	*The Cement Tent.*	Mahwah, N.J.: Troll, 1970. Boys solve the problem of a tent that just won't stay up.	B
Feature: Can be used to predict what reader would do to solve the problem.			
Cutting, B. and J.	*Are You a Ladybug?*	San Diego, Calif.: Wright Group, 1988. Ladybug searches for another ladybug, but other creatures just don't match up until the end.	B
Feature: Can be used to discuss animal characteristics.			
Greydanus, R.	*Let's Get a Pet.*	Mahwah, N.J.: Troll, 1988. Children learn the responsibilities and the pleasures of having a pet.	C
Feature: Especially good for short *e* words.			
Keats, E.	*Over in the Meadow.*	New York: Scholastic, 1971. Rhythmic verses describe life in the meadow.	C
Feature: Use to discuss action words.			

Author	Title	Information	
Melser, J. and Cowley, J.	*Obadiah.*	New York: Wright Group, 1980. Traditional rhyme describes Obadiah's adventure.	C
Feature: Can be used as a basis for additional couplet work.			

Personal Additions:

Sample Lesson— CVC Short Vowel Rule

Book:

Dan, the Flying Man

Introduction:

"What do you think was in the packet on Dan's back that made him fly?" Discuss. "As we were reading this story I noticed something about the words *Dan, ran, can.* Does anyone else see anything special about those words?" Discuss that they rhyme, that they end the same, that the only difference is the beginning letter and any other feature the children may notice about the words.

Lesson:

"You know students, many times when words have only one vowel in the middle that vowel will make its short sound. Does the *a* make its short sound in *Dan, ran,* and *can?*" [yes] "Does anyone have another word that rhymes with *Dan, ran,* and *can?*" [*fan, tan, pan, man . . .*]

"Let's look at all those words and see if they follow the same rule." [yes]

"We can use that rule with many of the words we meet in stories or need to use when we write. Two favorite words of mine that follow that rule are *dad* and *mom.*" Discuss why.

"The next time you come across a word that has only one vowel between two consonants see if it follows the rule we talked about today; sometimes it won't, but many times it will."

"Now, let's look back at *Dan, the Flying Man* and find the words that follow this short vowel rule."

State generalization:

When there is only one vowel between two consonants, it is usually short.

Follow-up activity:

Have cards available that contain initial and ending consonant(s) with a blank in the middle. Children can place vowels that are printed on small tiles or tagboard squares in the middle of the card to see if a short-vowel word is formed. Example: p____ck would become a short-vowel word if an *a, i,* or *e* were placed in the middle. Encourage children to think of a sentence using that word to emphasize word meaning and not just the utterance of letter sounds.

Long Vowel CVVC Pattern

When two vowels appear together in a word, the first one is usually long and the second one is silent.

Examples:

rain	seat	boat
day	read	oak
	feet	snow

Writing/Spelling Connection

Long vowel sounds are usually easier to hear than short vowels; the exception may be the long sound of *u* because it is not pronounced exactly like the letter name *u.* Children can learn that when a long vowel sound is heard, the vowel usually is accompanied by another vowel somewhere in that word or syllable. They may not always choose the correct partner vowel, but the idea of having the second vowel will help them distinguish between writing *mad* for *made* or *ran* for *rain.*

Bibliographic Information and Annotations

Author	Title	Information	Level
Butler, A.	*The Bean Bag That Mom Made.*	Crystal Lake, Ill.: Rigby, 1984. Verse relates cumulative series of events that follow getting a new bean bag.	A
Feature: Relate to other cyclical stories, such as Cowley's *No, No.*			
Butler, A.	*Tommy's Tummy Ache.*	Crystal Lake, Ill.: Rigby, 1989. Tommy enjoys lots of junk food, but pays the price.	A
Feature: Can be used to discuss the comma; relate to health unit.			

Author	Title	Information	Level
Cowley, J.	*Feet.*	San Diego, Calif.: Wright Group, 1988. Feet can do all kinds of things for you!	A
Feature: Can be used as basis for discussion on what hands can do; what similar things, what different things.			
Cowley, J.	*Good for You.*	San Diego, Calif.: Wright Group, 1987. Popular character, Huggles, tops the list of things that are good for you.	A
Feature: Easy pattern to use as a model for a class book.			
Cowley, J.	*Long, Long Tail.*	San Diego, Calif.: Wright Group, 1986. Two dolls follow a tail until they find its source—the cat.	A
Feature: Can be used to discuss the concept of a mystery story.			
Krauss, R.	*Bears.*	New York: Harper & Row, 1948. Fictional bears engage in all kinds of rhyming activities.	A
Feature: Can be used to extend long-vowel rhyming patterns.			
Nash, P.	*The Tree.*	Cleveland, Ohio: Modern Curriculum Press, 1983. Basic concepts about trees.	A
Feature: Nonfiction book; relate to science unit on plants; especially good for working with *ee* pattern.			
Williams, R.	*What's Going On?*	Cypress, Calif.: Creative Teaching Press, 1994. Birthday sensations are experienced through the five senses.	A
Feature: Relate to science unit on the senses.			
Belanger, C.	*I Like the Rain.*	San Diego, Calif.: Wright Group, 1988. Weather vocabulary is presented within the context of a song.	B
Feature: Accompanying tape available; relate to science unit.			
Gordon, S.	*Now I Know Trees.*	Mahwah, N.J.: Troll, 1983. Colorful illustrations and simple text discuss the different kinds of trees and their life cycles.	B
Feature: Nonfiction; relate to books or poems about the seasons.			
Saksie, J.	*The Seed Song.*	Cypress, Calif.: Creative Teaching Press, 1994. Once seeds receive what they need, they grow.	B
Feature: Accompanying tape available; relate to science unit.			
Shaw, N.	*Sheep in a Jeep.*	Boston: Houghton Mifflin, 1986. Sheep must sell their jeep after a disastrous outing.	B
Feature: Especially good for *ee* and *ea* patterns; also *sh* digraph.			
Braithwaite, A.	*Ladybugs.*	New York: Franklin Watts, 1990. Accurate drawings support text about the life cycle of a ladybug.	C
Feature: Nonfiction; relate to Cutting's *Are You a Ladybug?*			

Author	Title	Information	Level
Jorgensen, G.	*Crocodile Beat.*	Crystal Lake, Ill.: Rigby, 1988. Rhythmic verse relates story of a crocodile who intends to spoil the celebration of other jungle animals.	C
Feature: Accompanying tape available; good for dramatization.			
Keats, E.	*Over in the Meadow.*	New York: Scholastic, 1971. Rhythmic verse presents life in the meadow.	C
Feature: Presents number words; relate to math concepts.			
Yolen, J.	*Owl Moon.*	New York: Scholastic, 1988. Child and father experience owling on a moonlit night.	C
Feature: Caldecott Medal winner.			

Personal Additions:

Sample Lesson—CVVC Long Vowel Rule

Note:

This vowel rule is often explained as "When two vowels go walking, the first one does the talking." That works as a mnemonic for some children, but may confuse others. If you notice children are having a hard time remembering this rule, simplify the explanation to something like "When *o* and *a* are together, *o* says 'oh,' and *a* says nothing."

Book:

Sheep in a Jeep

Introduction:

"How many of you would like to ride with those sheep?" Take some time for children to share their reactions.

"I noticed there were a lot of words that had a long *e* sound in that story. Who can name some?" List words in a *ee* column and a *ea* column.

"Does anyone notice anything similar about all these words?" Discuss. Direct children's attention to the fact that all the words have two vowels together, with *e* being the first vowel.

Lesson:

"There are many words in the English language that have two vowels together. When that occurs, the first vowel often makes the long sound, or says its own name, and the second vowel is silent; it doesn't say anything at all. Look at these words."

Present a chart or write on board: sail, boat, day.

Discuss how each word follows the new rule; ask children to supply rhyme words for each and list their words beneath the given word; accept only actual words and ask the children to use their words in a sentence to assure meaning.

State generalization:

"All these words follow the rule that says when there are two vowels in a word, the first one is long and the second one is silent."

Final example:

"Let's go back and count how many long-vowel words are in the story *Sheep in a Jeep*."

Follow-up activity:

From books shared with the class write words that follow the CVVC rule on individual cards. Allow partners to work with the cards; one child explains how the vowels will sound (in this word the *o* will say *o* and the *a* will say nothing) and says the word (*goat*), and the other child uses the word in a sentence. Then both children work together to find the word in the book (cards can have title or some other code on them so children know in which book to look), read the sentence the word is in, and talk about other clues in the story that help them know the word (pictures, patterns, what makes sense).

Long Vowel CVCe Pattern

When *e* is the final vowel in a word, the preceding vowel is usually long.

Examples:

ate	wire	robe	tube
cape	kite	hope	cute

Writing/Spelling Connection

Adding a final *e* to achieve a long vowel sound is one of those rules that children will overgeneralize; displaying lists of word families will help them distinguish among the various ways long vowel sounds can be written. For example, under the long sound of *a*, list words they may need in their writing that are spelled with the same pattern as *cake*, *rain*, *play*, and *weight*.

The word *have* is a word frequently used in children's writing and is an exception to the final *e* rule. However, *have* does follow another rule of English words: no English word ends in a *v*. The final *e* in the case of the word *have* serves a different purpose. Explaining that rule to the children often eliminates their spelling *have* as *hav*.

Bibliographic Information and Annotations

Author	Title	Information	Level
Cowley, J.	*My Home.*	San Diego, Calif.: Wright Group, 1986. Everyone likes his or her home, but the astronaut has a special reason for liking hers.	A
Feature: Relate to Hoberman's poem, "A House Is a House for Me."			
Cowley, J.	*Our Granny.*	San Diego, Calif.: Wright Group, 1986. Children's grandmother does everything with gusto!	A
Feature: Discuss special features about grandparents.			
Frost, M.	*Jack-o-lantern.*	San Diego, Calif.: Wright Group, 1990. A pumpkin is used to make all kinds of faces, but its best use is to make a pumpkin pie.	A
Feature: Uses common feeling words; relate to Kachenmeister's *On Monday When It Rained.*			
Grey, J.	*Yummy, Yummy.*	Mahwah, N.J.: Troll, 1981. When the baker can't decide what cake to make, a wonderful delight is the result.	A
Feature: Contains recipe words; relate to measurement.			
Greydanus, R.	*Mike's New Bike.*	Mahwah, N.J.: Troll, 1980. Mike's little sister benefits when Mike outgrows his bike.	A
Feature: Easy to relate to personal experiences with siblings.			
Graves, K.	*Mom Can Fix Anything.*	Cypress, Calif.: Creative Teaching Press, 1994. Little girl models mom's practical skills and behavior.	A
Feature: Good for breaking stereotype of unhandy mother.			
Peters, S.	*The Rooster and the Weather Vane.*	Mahwah, N.J.: Troll, 1988. A rooster and a weather vane decide they both have important jobs to do.	A
Feature: Can be used to discuss the importance of different jobs and responsibilities.			
Raabe, J.	*I Like What I Am.*	Cleveland, Ohio: Modern Curriculum Press, 1981. Pam is happy with all that she can do.	A
Feature: Particularly emphasizes long *i* words.			
Williams, R.	*Let's Take Care of the Earth.*	Cypress, Calif.: Creative Teaching Press, 1994. Each animal shown in its natural habitat gives reasons to care for it.	A
Feature: Relate to nonfiction books describing animal habitats.			
Crawford, T.	*The Cement Tent.*	Mahwah, N.J.: Troll, 1970. Boys solve the problem of a tent that just won't stay up.	B
Feature: Good book for discussion of how problem could be solved.			

Author	Title	Information	Level
Guarino, D.	*Is Your Mama a Llama?*	New York: Scholastic, 1989. Delightful verse describes various animal mothers.	B
Feature: Strong rhyme component helps with prediction.			
Nash, P.	*The Snail.*	Cleveland, Ohio: Modern Curriculum Press, 1983. Describes various kinds of snails and their habitats.	B
Feature: Nonfiction; relate to Williams's *Let's Take Care of the Earth.*			
Mahy, M.	*My Wonderful Aunt: Story 2.*	San Diego, Calif.: Wright Group, 1986. Continued adventures of eccentric aunt who enjoys life to the fullest.	B
Feature: Relate to Cowley's *Our Granny.*			
Bennett, J.	*Teeny Tiny.*	Boston: Houghton Mifflin, 1989. Picking up a bone in the churchyard causes big trouble for a teeny tiny woman.	C
Feature: Good for comparing different versions; there are about four versions of this tale.			
McKibben, R.	*The Big Enormous Turnip.*	Denver, Co.: LINK, 1988. Russian folk tale about how a farmer finally pulled up an enormous turnip.	C
Feature: Cumulative pattern; good for sequencing lesson.			
Slobodkina, E.	*Caps for Sale.*	New York: Harper & Row, 1987. Peddler runs into real monkey business when trying to sell his caps.	C
Feature: Reinforces color words; great for dramatization.			
Wirth, B.	*Margie and Me.*	New York: Four Winds Press, 1983. Girl finds a lost dog and is able to keep it.	C
Feature: Chapter book format, including a table of contents.			

Personal Additions:

Sample Lesson— CVCe Long Vowel Rule

Note:

There are many different names for final *e*. I have heard "dead e," "silent e," "quiet e," "magic e"; I have even heard teachers say that the final *e* "pinches the first vowel and makes it scream its own name." Use what you feel will make sense to your students, but be aware that too elaborate a story will complicate the issue for some and actually confuse them.

Book:

My Home

Introduction:

"Would you like a home that could fly? What is something special about your home?" Discuss.

"One of the sentences in our story is *I like my home*. I'm going to write that on the board. When we read this sentence, we know not to say 'I lick my home' because that just wouldn't make sense. But now I want you to look at this sentence: *I like ice cream*." Write sentence on board.

"Does *I like ice cream* make sense?" [Sure.]

"Does *I lick ice cream* make sense?" [Yes, that makes sense too.]

"How can we tell whether the word is *lick* or *like*?" See what children have to say.

Lesson:

"The letter *e* has a special part to play in many of the words we read and write. By adding an *e* to the end of a short-vowel word, we can often make a new word. Let's read this list of words together: *fin, can, hop, us*."

"Watch what happens if I add an *e* to the end of those words."

Read the new words with the students. Discuss how adding the final *e* changed the sound of the short vowel to a long vowel.

Allow children time to practice with additional words: *rob, dim, can, hid, cut, tap, not, tub*.

List words with the final *e* and allow children to cover it up and change the word to a short-vowel word.

State generalization:

"So we can see that when a word has a final *e*, the first vowel is usually long and the *e* is silent."

Final example:

"Look at the title of this book." Show *Caps for Sale*.

"If I saw that sign in a store, I might think it said 'capes for Sal,' but knowing the silent *e* rule helps me to know that it is *caps*, not *capes*, that are for *sale*, not for *Sal*."

Follow-up activity:

Display a poster with short-vowel words followed by a small square of Velcro®. Back small squares of tagboard with Velcro and mark a lower case *e* on the other side. Children can practice changing long-vowel words to short-vowel words, or vice versa, by either adding or deleting the final *e*.

Short Vowel VC Pattern

When a single vowel is at the beginning of a word it is usually short.

Examples:

at	etch	in	on	up
ask	egg	if	odd	us

Writing/Spelling Connection

Short-vowel sounds at the very beginning of a word often are easier for children to hear than when they are in the middle of a word. These words provide good practice in establishing what the short vowel sound is. Be aware of common changes in pronunciation, such as saying *egg* with a long *a* sound at the beginning. You may not wish to use *egg* as an example, if your students pronounce it with a long *a* sound.

These short-vowel words can be used to demonstrate "stretching" words to hear each sound. The vowel sounds can be sustained, and only one or two final sounds need to be added. Practicing "stretching" these simple words develops the phonemic awareness and verbal skills needed to accurately spell more elaborate words. Being able to sequentially segment sounds is important to the progress in both reading and writing.

Bibliographic Information and Annotations

Author	Title	Information	Level
Berenstain, S. and J.	*Inside Outside Upside Down.*	New York: Random House, 1968. Little Bear has an adventure when he gets trapped in a box.	A
Feature: Uses directional words and opposites.			
Cowley, J.	*The Bicycle.*	San Diego, Calif.: Wright Group, 1983. A bicycle holds several circus performers—almost!	A
Feature: Repeats short *o* in beginning and middle of words.			
Cowley, J.	*Huggles Can Juggle.*	San Diego, Calif.: Wright Group, 1986. Popular Huggles juggles all kinds of food.	A
Feature: Good book for introducing the use of *an* instead of *a* in words that begin with a vowel.			
Cowley, J.	*Mouse.*	San Diego, Calif.: Wright Group, 1983. A mouse finally reaches the cheese.	A
Feature: Uses direction words.			
Jordan, S.	*Kittens.*	San Diego, Calif.: Wright Group, 1988. Grandma's kittens are everywhere!	A
Feature: Relate to Ward's *Cookie's Week.*			
Lawrence, L.	*What Can Fly?*	Crystal Lake, Ill.: Rigby, 1989. Presents things that can and cannot fly.	A
Feature: Can be used to discuss different ways to categorize; relate to Gelman's *Why Can't I Fly?*			
Masters, C.	*Kangaroo's Umbrella.*	Cleveland, Ohio: Modern Curriculum Press, 1984. Everyone thinks kangaroo is silly until it starts to rain.	A
Feature: Relate to Lionni's *Frederick.*			
Min, L.	*Mrs. Sato's Hens.*	Glenview, Ill.: Scott Foresman, 1994. Child helps Mrs. Sato count eggs until one day she finds chicks to count.	A
Feature: Reinforces names of the days of the week.			
Everett, L.	*Bubble Gum in the Sky.*	Mahwah, N.J.: Troll, 1978. Lou's bubble gum takes him on quite an adventure.	B
Feature: Relate to Gregorich's *The Gum on the Drum.*			
Gordon, S.	*Easter Bunny's Lost Egg.*	Mahwah, N.J.: Troll, 1980. Easter Bunny finds a surprise when he finds his lost egg.	B
Feature: Relate to Min's *Mrs. Sato's Hens.*			
Kim, J.	*Come On Up!*	Mahwah, N.J.: Troll, 1981. Lucy finds a reason to join her friends in the tree.	B
Feature: Some text appears in conversation bubbles.			

Author	Title	Information	Level
Drew, D.	*Tadpole Diary.*	Crystal Lake, Ill.: Rigby, 1987. Photographs support the text, which records the stages from tadpole to frog.	C
Feature: Nonfiction; relate to science unit on amphibians.			

Personal Additions:

Sample Lesson—
VC Short Vowel Rule

Note:

Once children are familiar with monosyllabic words that begin with a single vowel, show them how the rule can apply to words of more than one syllable. Being able to say the first syllable of a word often is all that is needed for the reader to realize the whole word. Some examples might be words like: *after, enter, important, October, under.*

Book:

Come On Up!

Introduction:

"Why did Lucy finally decide to join her friends in the tree?" Discuss.

"*On* and *up* are two words in the title of this story. I have listed those and some other little words on the board." List: *at, in, it, and, off, us.*

"What is at the beginning of all these words?" [one vowel]

"Is there a short-vowel or a long-vowel sound?" [short]

Lesson:

"When a vowel is by itself at the beginning of a word, it is usually short."

"I have three books we have already heard for each group. Look through the books and see what words you can find that follow this rule. When you find a word, have someone come to the board and list it under the right column." Have columns for each vowel.

Discuss the list, emphasizing the difference in short vowel sounds by pointing out the differences between *on* and *in* and other pairs.

Often these two- and three-letter words become easily recognized by sight, which is good. Help children to see how using that knowledge can help them when reading or writing unknown words.

When they want to write a word that starts with the sound of "ah" for example, they might think of the word *on* and try using an *o*.

State generalization:

"When a vowel is by itself at the beginning of a word, it is usually short."

Follow-up activity:

The activity described is an adaptation of the Elkonin boxes described in chapter 7 of *Partners in Learning: Teachers and Children in Reading Recovery* by DeFord, Lyons, and Pinnell (1993). Not all children need instruction in phonemic awareness, and those children who easily hear and reproduce isolated sounds should not be made to engage in this type of activity; however, it can be powerful for those students struggling with hearing sounds in sequence. It is included with this lesson because words of only two or three sounds, and especially words in which initial sounds can be easily sustained, are best for introducing this procedure. If demonstrating this to a group, an overhead projector may be used. If working with only one to three children, this may be done on a paper in front of them.

Procedure for the word *and*: Have three coins or beans.

"Children, I'm going to say the word *and*; each time I hear a different sound, I'm going to move a marker." Say *and* slowly, but with a continuous flow of speech; don't stop after each sound. As you say the short *a*, move a marker; then move one as you say the sound of *n*, and the third as you say the sound of *d*.

"How many sounds are there in *and*?" Repeat if children did not understand that there are three sounds.

"Right. Now I'm going to mark three lines on this paper (or transparency); as I say each sound, I'm going to move the marker onto the line."

Demonstrate several times, then have children do it individually; you may need to direct their hands for beginning tries.

This technique can be used for any word that is phonetically reliable. Do remember to mark lines for each sound, not each letter. For example, *that* would have only three lines because *th* is one sound. Once children consistently hear the sounds, they may be asked to write the letters on the line. Use a longer line, or a dotted line, for digraphs like *th*, but maintain one line per sound, not letter. I've used a dotted box as a code for a silent *e*. When assisting children in writing, I have given them only the number of sounds a word has and let them fill in the lines on their own. They get quite good at it once they have learned to stretch words and hear individual sounds. One first-grade student successfully wrote *grandpa* by just being told there were seven sounds in the word.

Long Vowel CV Pattern

When a single vowel is at the end of a word, it is often long.

Examples:

be	go	hi
she	so	gnu
we	no	
me	yo-yo	

Writing/Spelling Connection

With the exception of *gnu*, of course, most children correctly spell words like the above examples almost naturally once they are able to hear the individual sounds. This particular rule is best presented after children have reached that stage. Build on their knowledge of one word to explain others that follow the same pattern. Nearly every first grader I have taught knows "N-O spells NO!" That is a good starting point for learning *go* and *so*. Likewise, "M-E spells me" can be used to learn *be*, *we*, *he* and *she*.

Bibliographic Information and Annotations

Author	Title	Information	Level
Avitabile, R.	*When Lana Was Absent.*	Crystal Lake, Ill.: Rigby, 1988. Everyone notices when Lana is absent—and when she returns!	A
Feature: Relate to Wells's *Noisy Nora*.			
Cowley, J.	*Spider, Spider.*	San Diego, Calif.: Wright Group, 1987. After trying to come to her tea, spider turns down an invitation by bird.	A
Feature: Can be used to introduce food chain concept in science.			
Peters, S.	*The Rooster and the Weather Vane.*	Mahwah, N.J.: Troll, 1988. The rooster and the weather vane decide that they both have important jobs to do.	A
Feature: Relate to Cowley's *I'm Bigger Than You.*			
Craig, J.	*Little Danny Dinosaur.*	Mahwah, N.J.: Troll, 1988. Little Danny discovers that sometimes little is best.	B
Feature: Relate to Aesop's fable of the lion and the mouse.			
Everett, L.	*Bubble Gum in the Sky.*	Mahwah, N.J.: Troll, 1988. Lou's bubble gum takes him on quite an adventure.	B
Feature: Relate to Gregorich's *The Gum on the Drum.*			
Kim, J.	*Come On Up!*	Mahwah, N.J.: Troll, 1981. Lucy finds a reason to join her friends in the tree.	B
Feature: Some text appears in conversation bubbles.			
Everett, L.	*Skating on Thin Ice.*	Mahwah, N.J.: Troll, 1988. Rosie proves to be a good skater and a true friend.	C
Feature: Can use phrase "skating on thin ice" to discuss idioms.			
McClintock, M.	*A Fly Went By.*	New York: Random House, 1958. Everyone is running in circles because of a fly.	C
Feature: Relate to Cowley's *No, No.*			
McKissack, P.	*Three Billy Goats Gruff.*	Chicago: Regensteiner, 1987. Rendition of the classic tale.	C
Feature: Relate to other fairy tales and other versions of this story.			

Personal Additions:

Sample Lesson—
CV Long Vowel Pattern:

Note:

Since most of the words following this rule are easily learned by children, I would present this rule after the children have demonstrated sight recognition of some of the words. Rather than emphasizing using this rule to decode a word like *go* or *me*, I would bring it to their attention that *go* and *me* are words that fall into this category.

Book:

Spider, Spider

Introduction:

"Why didn't spider want to go to bird's tea party?" Discuss.

"Did anyone hear a rhyme in this story?" [tea and me] Discuss that they both have the long *e* sound at the end.

Lesson:

"Let's look at those words. We have talked about *e* and *a* being partners to make the sound of long *e*. Notice that *e* by itself also makes the sound of long *e*. Will that always be true if *e* is by itself?" Discuss.

State generalization:

"So if *e* is by itself at the beginning of a word, it usually makes a short *e* sound, like in the name *Ed*, but, if *e* is by itself at the end of a word, it most often will make a long *e* sound, like in the word *me*. A vowel by itself at the end of a word will often have a long sound."

Final example:

What other words that you know follow that rule?" [so, no, go, be . . .] List.

Follow-up activity:

Have a deck of cards containing two- or three-letter words that begin with a short vowel sound (and, is, ask, ill, up, on, Ed, etch . . .), and two- or three-letter words that end with a long vowel sound (be, go, hi, me, she, so, we, no . . .). Have children sort cards by the position of the vowel, then turn the cards in each pile upside down, so the words cannot be seen. The children take turns choosing a card from one of the piles, reading the word, and using the word in a sentence.

Y as a Vowel

When **y** is at the end of a one-part word, it has the sound of long *i*; when **y** is at the end of a two-part word, it has the sound of long *e*.

Examples:

my	happy
sky	party
why	noisy

Writing/Spelling Connection

Remind the children that **y** can be both a consonant and a vowel. When **y** is at the beginning of a word, it is a consonant, as in the words *yellow*, *yard*, and *yo-yo*. When **y** is at the end of a word, it is a vowel and will either make the sound of long *i* or long *e*. You can help children learn the **y** *as long i rule* by making them aware that very few words they will read or write end with the letter *i*. That long *i* sound is usually made by using the vowel **y**. Most children will spell *happy* or *funny* as *hape*, *fune*. You can help them see that adding a final *e* often indicates that you wish the first vowel to be long and the *e* silent. A long *e* sound at the end of a word is more commonly made by using the vowel **y**.

Bibliographic Information and Annotations

Author	Title	Information	Level
Butler, A.	*Teeny Tiny Tina.*	Crystal Lake, Ill.: Rigby, 1989. Everything is teeny in Teeny Tiny Tina's house.	A
Feature: Variation in print; some words are smaller than others; emphasizes *y* as long *e*.			
Cowley, J.	*My Puppy.*	San Diego, Calif.: Wright Group, 1986. Mother dog lets the rest of the family know just whose puppy it is.	A
Feature: Emphasizes *y* both as long *i* and as long *e*.			

Author	Title	Information	Level
Gaulke, G.	*Where Is My Shoe?*	New York: Holt, Rinehart & Winston, 1965. Little girl asks different animals if they have found her shoe.	A
Feature: Good for discussing concept of *pairs*; emphasizes *y* as long *e*.			
Gordon, S.	*The Jolly Monster.*	Mahwah, N.J.: Troll, 1988. Seeing his face in a mirror finally makes Wally laugh.	A
Feature: Emphasizes *y* as long *e*.			
Gruber, S.	*The Monster Under My Bed.*	Mahwah, N.J.: Troll, 1985. There *is* something under the bed, but it's hardly a monster!	A
Feature: Relate to Mayer's books *There's a Nightmare in My Closet, There's Something in My Attic,* and *There's an Alligator Under My Bed*; emphasizes *y* as long *e*.			
Lawrence, L.	*I Spy.*	Crystal Lake, Ill.: Rigby, 1989. Puppy spies all his animal friends.	A
Feature: Emphasizes *y* as long *i*; can be used as a basis for "I Spy" using books in which you look for certain word features.			
Neville, P., and Butler, A.	*Breakfast in Bed.*	Crystal Lake, Ill.: Rigby, 1984. Breakfast in bed may be messy, but it's fun.	A
Feature: Emphasizes *y* as long *e*.			
Dabcovich, L.	*Busy Beavers.*	New York: Scholastic, 1988. Beavers are so busy, they almost get caught by the fox.	B
Feature: Emphasizes *y* as long *e*; presents factual information about how beavers prepare their homes.			
Damon, L.	*Birthday Buddies.*	Mahwah, N.J.: Troll, 1988. Buddy gets the perfect birthday gift for grandpa.	B
Feature: Emphasizes *y* as both long *i* and long *e*; can use to model question and answer format in writing.			
de Regniers, S.	*What Did You Put in Your Pocket?*	New York: Scott Foresman, 1989. Cumulative verse about what a kangaroo puts in its pocket.	B
Feature: Emphasizes *y* as long *e*; relate to marsupial unit.			
Eggleton, J.	*Visitors.*	Crystal Lake, Ill.: Rigby, 1988. Fair-weather friends join in fun times, but not in bad.	B
Feature: Emphasizes *y* as long *e*; introduce a hyphen; discuss friendship; relate to Everett's *Skating on Thin Ice.*			
Hutchins, P.	*The Surprise Party.*	New York: Aladdin Books, 1991. Rabbit's news about his party gets mixed up as it spreads from one animal to another.	B
Feature: Emphasizes *y* as long *e*; discuss listening skills; play "Telephone," where one message is whispered from one child to the next and the last child repeats what he or she heard.			

Author	Title	Information	Level
Irons, Calvin.	*Hurry Hurry.*	Crystal Lake, Ill.: Rigby, 1990. Turtles hurry as they watch the clock and get ready for school—on Saturday!	B
Feature: Emphasizes *y* as long *e*; rhyme can be used for prediction.			
Melser, J.	*Yes Ma'am.*	San Diego, Calif.: Wright Group, 1980. Boy helps out with farm animals, but ends up head over heels.	B
Feature: Introduce apostrophe in *ma'am*; emphasizes *y* as long *e*.			
Neville, P., and Butler, A.	*Green Bananas.*	Crystal Lake, Ill.: Rigby, 1984. Fruit salad is best when made with green bananas.	B
Feature: Emphasizes *y* as long *e*; relate to health unit and make fruit salad!			
Van Allen, R.	*A Dream in a Wishing Well.*	Allen, Tex.: DLM Teaching Resources, 1985. Money may limit what we can buy, but dreams have no limits.	B
Feature: Emphasizes *y* as both long *i* and long *e*; relate to unit on money, especially pennies.			
Craig, J.	*Here Comes Winter.*	Mahwah, N.J.: Troll, 1988. Billy's shopping spree prepares him for the coming winter.	C
Feature: Emphasizes *y* as long *e*; use for sequencing activity.			
Hillman, J.	*Chicken Little.*	Hawthorn, Australia: Mimosa, 1989. Traditional version of the classic tale.	C
Feature: Emphasizes *y* as both long *i* and long *e*; dialogue is color coded.			
Kellogg, S.	*Chicken Little.*	Boston: Houghton Mifflin, 1989. Classic tale retold with a modern twist.	C
Feature: Emphasizes *y* as both long *i* and long *e*; relate to traditional versions.			
Wing, H.	*Ten Pennies for Candy.*	New York: Holt, Rinehart & Winston, 1963. Ten pennies buys just enough candy for all of Sandy's "friends".	C
Feature: Emphasizes *y* as long *e*; relate to money unit.			

Personal Additions:

Sample Lesson—
Y as a Vowel Rule

Note:

Be sure children have had practice in clapping out, or somehow counting out syllables. I use the phrases "how many parts" and "how many syllables" interchangeably. Again, names are a great tool for learning about syllables because children understand that "Melissa" is only one word, but three parts can be heard. As children become more advanced, you can point out that each syllable must have a vowel.

Book:

My Puppy

Introduction:

"How many different words are in the story, *My Puppy*?" [three]

"Isn't it interesting to think that you can write a story with only three words! Two of those words have the letter *y* in them. Which two?" [*my, puppy*]

"I'm going to use those two words to start a sentence." Write: *My puppy is yellow.*

"How many words have the letter *y* in this sentence?" [three]

"Yes, there are three words with the letter *y*, but *y* says something different in all three of them. Let's look at those words." Discuss.

Lesson:

"Remember that *y* can be either a consonant or a vowel. What determines the job it will do is where it comes in the word. Where does *y* come in the word *yellow*?" [beginning]

"When *y* comes at the beginning of a word it is a consonant and makes the sound we hear in words like *yard*, *yes*, *yo-yo,* and *yarn.* Now let's look at what happens to *y* when it is at the end of a word."

Discuss that *y* is a vowel when it is at the end of a word, and whether or not it says long *i* or long *e* depends on how many parts or syllables the word has.

"How many parts in *my*?" [one]

"When *y* comes at the end of a one-part word it makes the sound of long *i*. How many parts in puppy?" [two]

"When *y* comes at the end of a two-part word it makes the sound of long *e*."

Allow the children to work in pairs; give each pair a word with *y* as a vowel. The partners decide what the word is, share it with the class, use it in a sentence, and explain which part of the *y* rule their word follows.

"One of my favorite words with *y* as a vowel is the word *happy*. Can anyone find that word in our room?" [perhaps on Happy Birthday chart]. "There will be many words with *y* that you will meet when you read and that you will want to use when you write. See if knowing the rule about *y* will help you with some of those words."

State generalization:

When **y** is at the end of a one-part word, it has the sound of long *i*; when **y** is at the end of a two-part word, it has the sound of long *e*.

Follow-up activity:

Have a set of sentences written on tagboard that omit the final letter *y*. For example: *The bird is happ- when it can fl-.; M- bab- sister is sill-.; I hope it is sunn-, not rain-, for our picnic.; Sall- will tr- to hold the bunn-.* Laminate the tagboard so the sentences can be used repeatedly. Allow children to practice inserting the letter *y* with erasable markers. Either have them read the finished sentence aloud to check for comprehension, or ask them to illustrate the sentence they have completed.

Consonant Blends

When two or more consonants appear together and each consonant can be heard in sequence, there is a consonant blend.

Examples:

r-blends	l-blends	s-blends
tree	block	swing
print	plant	spell
green	glue	smile
frog	flag	spring
dress	class	strike
crack	sleep	ski

Writing/Spelling Connection

Many children omit the second or third letter of a blend when they are reading or writing a word. An excellent activity for helping children hear and represent all the consonant sounds of a blend is the Elkonin procedure described in the follow-up activity for the short vowel VC pattern (see chapter 2). If using this procedure, be sure a line is designated for each letter of the blend;

blends are not represented by one line because each sound can be heard in a consonant blend.

Tr and *dr* blends cause particular difficulty for spellers still using the point of articulation to decide what letter(s) to use to represent a sound. The beginning sound of *dragon* is made much the same way as the sound we make when we say the letter *j*. For the same reason, children who learn the *ch* digraph will often use that to begin the word *tree* or *train*. Using Elkonin to help children articulate the *tr* and *dr* blends while showing them visual examples of the words will reinforce those blend patterns.

Bibliographic Information and Annotations

Author	Title	Information	Level
Cowley, J.	*Little Brother.*	San Diego, Calif.: Wright Group, 1986. Story relays baby's antics in a highchair.	A
Feature: Presents *r* and *l* blends; use of comma.			
Cowley, J.	*Stop!*	San Diego, Calif.: Wright Group, 1982. It takes quite a crash to finally stop a runaway truck.	A
Feature: Presents *st* and *tr* blends.			
King, S.	*Baby's Dinner.*	San Diego, Calif.: Rigby, 1989. Baby plays with food and ends up in the tub.	A
Feature: Presents *sp*, *pl*, *sl*, and *spl* blends.			
Lawrence, L.	*Too Many Clothes.*	San Diego, Calif.: Rigby, 1989. After dressing up in Mom's and Dad's clothes, child decides it's best without any!	A
Feature: Presents *sk*, *sc*, *sw* and *cl* blends; uses possessive *'s*.			
Melser, J., and Cowley, J.	*Three Little Ducks.*	San Diego, Calif.: Wright Group, 1980. Mother Duck teaches her three ducklings all they need to know to live in the pond.	A
Feature: Presents *fl*, *sl*, *cr*, *sw*, and *sn* blends.			
Rogers, P.	*What Will the Weather Be Like Today?*	New York: Scholastic, 1989. Animals describe what the perfect weather would be for them.	A
Feature: Presents *st*, *sk*, *sn*, *fr*, *cl*, *pl*, and *dr* blends; discuss what is "perfect weather" for you.			
Urmston, K., and Evans, K.	*The Marching Band.*	Cleveland, Ohio: Kaeden, 1991. Many instruments make up the marching band.	A
Feature: Presents *fl*, *pl*, *cl*, *tr*, and *dr* blends; play band music and discuss which of the instruments are heard.			
Buckley, C.	*The Greedy Gray Octopus.*	Crystal Lake, Ill.: Rigby, 1983. Greedy octopus meets his demise when he invites a shark to tea.	B
Feature: Presents *gr*, *cr*, *bl*, *squ*, and *pl* blends; relate to Cowley's *Spider, Spider.*			
Ehlert, L.	*Planting a Rainbow.*	San Diego, Calif.: Harcourt Brace Jovanovich, 1988. Vivid illustrations add to this account of growing a colorful garden.	B
Feature: Presents *pl*, *gr*, *spr*, *fl*, *bl*, and *br* blends; reinforces color words.			

Author	Title	Information	Level
Gackenbach, D.	*Claude the Dog.*	New York: Clarion Books, 1974. A beloved dog shares his gifts with his less fortunate friends.	B
Feature: Presents *cl, fr, bl, pr, sl,* and *cr* blends.			
Granowsky, A.	*The Praying Mantis.*	Cleveland, Ohio: Modern Curriculum Press, 1983. Describes characteristics and habits of the praying mantis.	B
Feature: Nonfiction; presents *fl, fr, pl,* and *pr* blends; relate to science unit on insects.			
Greydanus, R.	*Now I Know Changing Seasons.*	Mahwah, N.J.: Troll, 1983. Animals adapt to each season of the year.	B
Feature: Presents *gr, pl, spr, tr, sk, br, sn,* and *str* blends; relate to Roger's *What Will the Weather Be Like Today?*			
King, S.	*Grandpa Snored.*	Crystal Lake, Ill.: Rigby, 1989. Nothing wakes up Grandpa—until Grandma turns off the TV.	B
Feature: Presents *sn, scr, pl, fl,* and *gr* blends; relate to Mayer's *Just Grandpa and Me.*			
Neitzel, S.	*The Jacket I Wear in the Snow.*	New York: Scholastic, 1989. Rebus format is used to present cumulative articles of winter clothing.	B
Feature: Presents *sn, st, sc, sw, sl, str,* and *sm* blends; relate to Lawrence's *Too Many Clothes.*			
Titherington, J.	*Pumpkin, Pumpkin.*	New York: Scholastic, 1989. Story presents stages from seed to harvested pumpkin.	B
Feature: Presents *spr, pl,* and *gr* blends; good for sequencing activity.			
Wandelmaler, R.	*Now I Know Clouds.*	Mahwah, N.J.: Troll, 1985. Describes different kinds of clouds and what kind of weather they indicate.	B
Feature: Nonfiction; presents *cl, sk, dr, fl, str, br, gr,* and *pl* blends; uses opposites.			
Aesop.	*The Exploding Frog.*	Cleveland, Ohio: Modern Curriculum Press, 1987. Frog suffers the consequences when he tries to be bigger than he is.	C
Feature: Presents *br, fr,* and *cr* blends; relate to other Aesop fables.			
Brett, J.	*Annie and the Wild Animals.*	Boston: Houghton Mifflin, 1985. Annie tries to find a new pet when her cat disappears.	C
Feature: Presents *sn, st, sl, str, pl, fr, sm, tr,* and *gr* blends; relate to Barchas's *I Was Walking Down the Road.*			
Flack, M.	*Ask Mr. Bear.*	New York: Collier Books, 1960. All the animals offer Danny a gift to give to his mother for her birthday. Mr. Bear offers the best gift of all.	C
Feature: Presents *st, sk, cl, fr, bl, tr,* and *thr* blends; relate to Cowley's *Good for You.*			

Author	Title	Information	Level
Gilman, P.	*Jillian Jiggs.*	New York: Scholastic, 1987. Jillian puts off cleaning her room until her mother insists it be done.	C

Feature: Presents blends with *r, t,* and *l*; relate to Shel Silverstein's poem "Messy Room" from *A Light in the Attic.*

Lobel, A.	*Frog and Toad Are Friends.*	New York: Harper & Row, 1970. Frog and Toad share their friendship and their many adventures.	C

Feature: Lobel's wonderful stories about Frog and Toad have many words that use consonant digraphs, chapter book format, including a table of contents.

Personal Additions:

Sample Lesson—Consonant Blends

Book:

The Marching Band

Introduction:

"Do any of you play an instrument?" Discuss.

"Name some instruments that were in our book." List on board, entering those instruments that begin with a consonant blend in one column. [flute, clarinet, trumpet, drum]

"Notice that in this column, all the names begin with two consonants together; let's say the names of these instruments slowly." Emphasize consonant blend.

"You can hear both of those letters, and each one is important in making the word."

Lesson: "What would happen if we took that second consonant away?" Allow children to have fun playing with the words. [drum becomes dum; flute becomes fute . . .]

"When two consonants come together and each one can be heard, it is called a consonant blend. Sometimes, there are three consonants, like in one of the words in this sentence." Write: *The band is marching down the street.*

"Who can find the word with a three-consonant blend and read the sentence for us?"

Present chart with various consonant blends; ask children to read the word, use it in a sentence, and circle the two or three letters that make the consonant blend.

State generalization:

When two or three consonants come together and each one can be heard, it is called a consonant blend.

Follow-up activity:

Perceiving consonant blends as a cluster of letters instead of two or three individual letters contributes to fluent reading and writing. Provide cards with pictures of objects whose names begin with various blends. Children name the two or three letters that form the blend, then check the back of the card for the right answer. A variation is to provide cards with just consonant blends printed on them (br, sl, tr, gl, dr, spr . . .). With a partner, allow children to fan cards like a deck, pick an unseen blend and think of a word that begins with that blend. The word must be used in a sentence to guard against children just uttering sounds. To extend this activity, have a "Book of Blends" available, listing the most common words likely to be used by the children. When the children guess a word, they can check in the blend book to see if it is there or to add their new word.

Consonant Digraphs

When two consonants appear together and make one sound, there is a consonant digraph. Examples:

th digraph	*sh* digraph	*wh* digraph	*ch* digraph
then	shop	white	chick
mother	washer	meanwhile	matches
teeth	fresh		such

Writing/Spelling Connection

It is important to have key words and pictures for the consonant digraphs because they are not easily remembered in isolation. *The* is one of the first sight words I teach my children because it is the word most often written in the English language. It becomes a good focus word for the *th* digraph. Displaying posters with sheep jumping over *Sh,* or whales swimming through *Wh,* or chicks pecking at *Ch* can be helpful too. Don't overlook the common occurrence of digraphs in the medial or final position of a word. Have a poster for each digraph on which there are three columns. List words with the digraph as the initial sound in the left column, words with the digraph in the medial position in the middle column, and words with the digraph in the final position in the right column.

Bibliographic Information and Annotations

Th Digraph

Author	Title	Information	Level
Gruber, S.	*The Monster Under My Bed.*	Mahwah, N.J.: Troll, 1985. There *is* something under the bed, but it is hardly a monster!	A
Feature: Uses onomatopoeia.			
Latham, R., and Sloan, P.	*Why Do Polar Bears Like the Arctic?*	Crystal Lake, Ill.: Rigby, 1988. Animals describe the climate each of them likes and wonder why the polar bear likes the Arctic.	A
Feature: Nonfiction; illustrations strongly support repeated pattern. Relate to Roger's *What Will the Weather Be Like Today?*			
Wang, M.	*The Ant and the Dove.*	Crystal Lake, Ill.: Rigby, 1989. Aesop tale tells how a little creature can help a more powerful one.	A
Feature: Relate to Craig's *Little Danny Dinosaur.*			
Flack, M.	*Ask Mr. Bear.*	New York: Collier Books, 1960. All the animals offer to give Danny a gift for his mother's birthday. Mr. Bear offers the best gift of all.	B
Feature: Relate to Cowley's *Good for You.*			
McKissack, P.	*Three Billy Goats Gruff.*	Chicago: Regensteiner, 1987. Traditional version of the classic tale.	B
Feature: Use to discuss the "threes" in fairy tales.			
Peters, S.	*The Tooth Fairy.*	Mahwah, N.J.: Troll, 1981. In spite of many questions, the tooth fairy remains a mystery.	B
Feature: Use of opposites.			
Allen, C.	*Carla's New Friends.*	Allen, Tex.: DLM Teaching Resources, 1987. Lonesome Carla finds new friends by using a carrot, some bread crumbs and an apple core.	C
Feature: Use to discuss what one needs to find a friend.			
Asch, F.	*Turtle Tale.*	New York: Scholastic, 1978. Turtle discovers that a wise turtle knows when to keep his head in or out of his shell.	C
Feature: Relate to nonfiction books about turtles and how shell is used for defense.			
Bailey, D.	*Butterflies and Moths.*	Austin, Tex.: National Education, 1990. Relates characteristics and habitats of butterflies and moths.	C
Feature: Nonfiction; discuss similarities and differences; relate to spiders and insects.			
Blegvad, L.	*Anna Banana and Me.*	Boston: Houghton Mifflin, 1989. Whimsical Anna helps her friend find source of bravery.	C
Feature: Use as basis for discussion about fears.			

Personal Additions:

Sh Digraph

Author	Title	Information	Level
Cowley, J.	*Mrs. Wishy Washy.*	San Diego, Calif.: Wright Group, 1980. Animals just can't resist that lovely mud.	A
Feature: Good example of digraph in medial position.			
Cowley, J.	*Shoo!*	San Diego, Calif.: Wright Group, 1986. Farm animals prefer a tasty garden, in spite of farmer's anger.	A
Feature: Relate to Cowley's *Mrs. Wishy-Washy.*			
Cowley, J.	*The Wind Blows Strong.*	San Diego, Calif.: Wright Group, 1987. The wind stirs up many sounds.	A
Feature: Uses onomatopoeia.			
King, S.	*Baby's Dinner.*	Crystal Lake, Ill.: Rigby, 1987. Baby plays with food and ends up in the tub.	A
Feature: Uses onomatopoeia.			
Parkes, B.	*Who's in the Shed?*	Crystal Lake, Ill.: Rigby, 1986. Peek-a-boo openings in pages make this mystery even more fun to read.	A
Feature: Encourages prediction.			
Buckley, C.	*The Greedy Gray Octopus.*	Crystal Lake, Ill.: Rigby, 1988. Greedy octopus meets his demise when he invites a shark to tea.	B
Feature: Relate to Cowley's *Spider, Spider.*			
Fowler, A.	*It Could Still Be a Fish.*	Chicago: Children's Press, 1990. Describes characteristics of unique and common fish.	B
Feature: Nonfiction; relate to Fowler's *It Could Still Be a Bird.*			
Robinson, W.	*If I Were a Fish.*	Allen, Tex.: DLM Teaching Resources, 1986. Different wishes bring different abilities.	B
Feature: Relate to Howe's *I Wish I Were a Butterfly.*			
Asch, F.	*Mooncake.*	New York: Scholastic, 1983. Bear thinks he has tasted the moon!	C
Feature: Relate to Greydanus's *Now I Know Changing Seasons.*			
Leonard, M.	*Bear's Busy Year.*	Mahwah, N.J.: Troll, 1990. Bear has fun through all four seasons.	C
Feature: Relate to nonfiction accounts of bears.			
Wilson, L.	*Summer Camp.*	Australia: Maubern, 1987. Even after a fun week at camp home is still best.	C
Feature: Relate to McKissack's *Country Mouse and City Mouse.*			

Personal Additions:

Wh Digraph

Author	Title	Information	Level
Cowley, J.	*"Scat!" Said the Cat.*	San Diego, Calif.: Wright Group, 1986. Each animal has a question to ask when the cat says "Scat!"	A
Feature: Rhyme can be used to help prediction; uses question words.			
Parkes, B.	*Who's In the Shed?*	Crystal Lake, Ill.: Rigby, 1986. Peek-a-boo openings in pages make this mystery even more fun to read.	A
Feature: Encourages prediction; strong use of rhyme.			
Peters, S.	*The Rooster and the Weather Vane.*	Mahwah, N.J.: Troll, 1988. The rooster and the weather vane decide that they both have important jobs to do.	A
Feature: Can be used to discuss the importance of different responsibilities.			
Rogers, P.	*What Will the Weather Be Like Today?*	New York: Scholastic, Animals respond to what would make the perfect weather for them.	A
Feature: Strong rhyme; uses comma and question mark; relate to Latham's and Sloan's *Why Do Polar Bears Like the Arctic?*			
Greydanus, R.	*Valentine's Day Grump.*	Mahwah, N.J.: Troll, 1981. Receiving valentines makes grumpy Gus happy.	B
Feature: Uses question words: *what* and *who*; uses comma and exclamation point.			
Kraus, R.	*Whose Mouse Are You?*	New York: Scholastic, 1970. Lonely mouse is reunited with his family.	B
Feature: Reinforces family names.			
Latham, R., and Sloan, P.	*Why Do Polar Bears Like the Arctic?*	Australia: Maubern, 1988. Animals discuss the climate each likes and wonder why the polar bear likes the Arctic.	B
Feature: Relate to Rogers's *What Will the Weather Be Like Today?*			
Peters, S.	*Now I Know Animals at Night.*	Mahwah, N.J.: Troll, 1983. Discusses several nocturnal animals.	B
Feature: Relate to Hutchins's *Good Night, Owl.*			
Blegvad, L.	*Anna Banana and Me.*	Boston: Houghton Mifflin, 1989. Whimsical Anna helps her friend find a source of bravery.	C
Feature: Can be used to discuss friendship and fears.			
Gackenbach, D.	*Harry and the Terrible Whatzit.*	New York: Scholastic, 1977. Harry overcomes his fear of the cellar when he thinks the terrible Whatzit has his mom.	C
Feature: Relate to Kim's *Come On Up!*			
Hayes, S.	*This Is the Bear.*	New York: Harper & Row, 1986. A boy finds his lost bear with the help of his dog.	C
Feature: Strong rhyme helps predict more difficult words; cumulative pattern.			

Personal Additions:

Ch Digraph

Author	Title	Information	Level
Cannard, E.	*Munching Mark.*	Crystal Lake, Ill.: Rigby, 1984. Mark's munching habits lead to a toothache.	A
Feature: Relate to Butler's *Tommy's Tummy Ache.*			
Cowley, J.	*Buzzing Flies.*	San Diego, Calif.: Wright Group, 1986. Flies buzz around lunch until they are finally chased out the door.	A
Feature: Rhyme helps with prediction.			
Cowley, J.	*Silly Old Possum.*	San Diego, Calif.: Wright Group, 1988. The fun begins when a possum falls down a chimney.	A
Feature: Uses directional words.			
Cowley, J.	*When Itchy Witchy Sneezes.*	San Diego, Calif.: Wright Group, 1986. Itchy Witchy has a magical sneeze.	A
Feature: Can be used in conjunction with health unit.			
Lawrence, L.	*Chew Chew Chew.*	Crystal Lake, Ill.: Rigby, 1989. Goats devour anything and everything.	A
Feature: Uses onomatopoeia.			
Neville, P.	*Hungry Horse.*	Crystal Lake, Ill.: Rigby, 1989. Horse insists on stopping for food in spite of "Giddy-up" command.	A
Feature: Good for reinforcing the sound of *h*.			
Gruber, S.	*Chatty Chipmunk's Nutty Day.*	Mahwah, N.J.: Troll, 1985. After searching everywhere for nuts, Chatty must decide where to hide them.	B
Feature: Closely related to factual information of a nonfiction book.			
Maccarone, G.	*Itchy, Itchy Chicken Pox.*	New York: Scholastic, 1992. Chicken pox runs its itchy course.	B
Feature: Relate to personal experiences with illness.			
Smith, J., and Parkes, B.	*Jack and the Beanstalk.*	Crystal Lake, Ill.: Rigby, 1988. Traditional version of the classic tale.	B
Feature: Reinforces use of quotation marks.			

Personal Additions:

Sample Lesson—
Consonant Digraphs

Note:

I would introduce each digraph separately, and I would allow enough time between lessons to assure that the digraph has been established. It is not imperative that the children learn to call these elements "digraphs"; it is more important that they can identify the sound made by each. The lesson below introduces the *sh* digraph. I have listed a good book to use for the introduction of each common digraph. Also, the sound of *f* can be made with either a *ph* or a *gh* digraph; *ph* is more commonly found at the beginning or middle of a word (*phone, elephant*), and *gh* is most often at the end of a word (*enough, laugh*). When children are familiar with the more common digraphs, you might consider introducing *ph* and *gh*.

Books:

sh—*Who's in the Shed?*; th—*The Monster Under My Bed*; wh—*Whose Mouse Are You?*; ch—*Chew Chew Chew*.

Introduction:

"Do you remember when we mixed paint together to make different colors? What happened when we mixed red and yellow?" [orange]

"How about blue and yellow?" [green]

"We had two different colors, and when we mixed them we got a whole new color. Well, sometimes letters do the same thing in words."

Lesson:

"Look at the words *shed* and *sheep* from our story *Who's in the Shed?* What sound do you hear at the beginning of both of those words?" [sh]

"Yes; it's like the sound we make when we tell people to be quiet, isn't it? We don't hear the sound *s* usually makes, and we don't hear the sound *h* usually makes. We hear a whole new sound. When two consonants are together and they make one new sound, that is called a consonant digraph. *Sh* is a consonant digraph because the *s* and the *h* go together and make one new sound. Were there any other words with an *sh* sound in our story *Who's In the Shed?*" Allow time for children to look for words.

"Let's think about words that have the *sh* sound." Write words on a chart or poster that

has three columns so words can be recorded as having the *sh* digraph in the initial, medial, or final positions.

Follow-up activity:

Play "Word Construction." Have a list of words with consonant digraphs in various positions within the words. Have children "construct" the words by using a different colored unifix cube for each sound. Digraphs must be represented by having two cubes of the same color snapped together. For example, the word *fish* might be a red cube next to a yellow cube next to two blue cubes snapped together. A variation is to have two or three words "constructed" and to have children try to see which words from a given list would match those patterns.

Final Sound of K

When a short-vowel word ends with the sound of *k*, use the *ck* digraph; when a long-vowel word ends with the sound of *k*, use *k* alone.

Examples:

tack	take
quick	bike
neck	week
rock	poke
luck	juke

Writing/Spelling Connection

When children begin asking "Is it a *c* or a *k*?", they are beginning to realize that spelling has a visual component that at times overrides the sound/letter relationship They are beginning to understand that words are spelled with specific letters, not just those that meet the auditory requirement. As soon as they begin asking about *c* and *k*, they become aware of some words that have both the *c and* the *k*. You begin seeing words like *macke* for *make* mixed in with *bic* for *bike*, and *bak* for *back*. Learning that if the word has a long vowel sound it most often will end with just the *k* helps with a lot of spelling decisions. In addition, simply telling children that *ck* is rarely followed by an *e* eliminates that possibility.

Bibliographic Information and Annotations

Author	Title	Information	Level
Cowley, J.	*The Farm Concert.*	San Diego, Calif.: Wright Group, 1989. Boisterous animals find way to have their concert and not keep the farmer awake.	A
Feature: Print variation denotes volume of voices.			
Cowley, J.	*Oh, Jump in a Sack.*	San Diego, Calif.: Wright Group, 1982. An escaped balloon meets its demise.	A
Feature: Uses hyphen.			
Isadora, R.	*I Hear.*	New York: Greenwillow Books, 1985. Children relate sounds they hear to various activities throughout the day.	A
Feature: Relate to unit on senses; use as a model for class "I See . . ." or "I Taste . . ." books.			
Melser, J., and Cowley, J.	*Three Little Ducks.*	San Diego, Calif.: Wright Group, 1980. Mother Duck teaches her three little ducks all they need to know to live in the pond.	A
Feature: Relate to Fowler's *It Could Still Be a Bird.*			
Randell, B.	*I Can Squeak.*	Portsmouth, N.H.: Heinemann, 1985. Specific sounds are characteristic of different animals.	A
Feature: Uses onomatopoeia.			
Williams, R.	*What's in My Pocket?*	Cypress, Calif.: Creative Teaching Press, 1994. Deductive thinking leads to what is in the pocket.	A
Feature: Relate to the game Twenty Questions.			
Blackman, M.	*Where's That Duck?*	Chicago: Children's Press, 1985. Animals follow a "quack" to a surprise fifth duck.	B
Feature: Relate to math concept of "one more."			
Brown, M.	*Pickle Things.*	New York: Parents Magazine Press, 1980. Humorous account of what pickles are *not* used for.	B
Feature: Theme can be adapted to write a class book.			
Elting, M., and Folsom, M.	*Q Is for Duck.*	New York: Clarion Books, 1980. Alphabet guessing game using common knowledge about animals and their habitats.	B
Feature: Excellent for practicing prediction skills.			
Van Allen, R.	*A Dream in a Wishing Well.*	Allen, Tex.: DLM Teaching Resources, 1985. Money may limit what we can buy, but dreams are boundless.	B
Feature: Relate to math unit on money, especially pennies.			

Author	Title	Information	Level
Vaughan, M.	*Hi-De-Hi.*	New York: Scott Foresman, 1994. Barnyard characters fill Uncle Marco's farm with noises.	B
Feature: Relate to Old MacDonald.			
Memling, C.	*Hi All You Rabbits.*	New York: Parents Magazine Press, 1970. Cumulative story about various animal actions.	C
Feature: Relate to Greydanus's *Animals at the Zoo*.			
Oppenheim, J.	*Have You Seen Birds?*	New York: Scholastic, Highly descriptive account of different kinds of birds.	C
Feature: Nonfiction; illustrations are done with clay; relate to Fowler's *It Could Still Be a Bird.*			

Personal Additions:

Sample Lesson— Final Sound of K

Note:

This lesson focuses on the ability to hear long and short vowel sounds, which determine the use of *k* alone or the *ck* digraph.

Book:

I Can Squeak

Introduction:

"I like the way the author used so many interesting words in that story. I especially liked squeak, croak, quack, and cluck. What were some of your favorite words?" Discuss.

"I noticed something else about some of the words in this story. I'm going to say a word, and I want you to tell me whether you hear a long vowel sound in that word or a short vowel sound." Say words; as children decide, print the words under a "long-vowel sound" column or a "short-vowel sound" column.

Lesson:

"Be word detectives now and see what you notice about these two lists of words." Discuss and lead children to the realization that the long-vowel words use only *k* for the final sound and that the short-vowel words use the *ck* digraph.

State generalization:

"When we're trying to decide whether to use a *c* or a *k* or a *ck* together, it helps to think of this: If a short-vowel word ends with a *k* sound, use *ck*; if a long-vowel word ends with a *k* sound, use *k* alone."

Final example:

"Now, I'm going to read some words on these cards; you tell me if the word uses just a *k* or a *ck*." Have selected words on cards (like, tack, bake, quick, week, track, joke, rock, make, sack . . .); allow children to guess as a group or individually, depending on their abilities. After they guess, show the card so they can see if their prediction was correct. If there is confusion, return to the explanation of the rule.

Follow-up activity:

Allow a group of three children to play "K Race." One child reads a word from a stack of cards; the other two see which one is the first to guess whether the word is spelled with a k or a ck. If the child is right, the card goes in his or her pile; if wrong, the other child gets the card (this discourages one child from guessing without thinking). The child with more cards wins the race. Mix the cards and change positions so the reader can be a race participant in the next round.

Diphthongs

When two vowels appear together and form an unsegmentable, varying, but single sound, there is a diphthong (also spelled *dipthong*).

Examples:

oy	oi	*ow*	ou	ew	oo (long)	*oo* (short)
boy	oil	how	house	knew	school	book
enjoy	point	brown	hour	drew	moon	good
toy	noise	down	out	few	tooth	rookie

Writing/Spelling Connection

Diphthongs are best learned by discovering word patterns. Focus on a meaningful word known by sight, such as *boy*. Make a word family chart listing all the common words that share the *oy* diphthong. Similar charts can be made for the other diphthongs. Key words most children find easy to recognize by sight are *oil, owl, new, school,* and *book*. The term *diphthong* is not one the children need to remember; what is important is the realization that two vowels work together to make a sound which is different from either one alone. The following bibliography concentrates on the *oi, oy, ou,* and *ow* diphthongs.

Bibliographic Information and Annotations

Author	Title	Information	Level
Berenstain, S. and J.	*Bears in the Night.*	New York: Random House, 1971. A "whoo" sends bears in all directions; then they must retrace their steps.	A
Feature: Relate to Carle's *The Secret Birthday Message.*			
Cowley, J.	*Down to Town.*	San Diego, Calif.: Wright Group, 1986. All the farmers' animals go to town.	A
Feature: Text can be adapted to tune of "Old MacDonald."			
Forbes, C.	*The Tree Stump.*	New York: Scott Foresman, 1994. Animals are enjoying hiding in a tree stump, until a porcupine enters!	A
Feature: Relate to the folk tale *The Mitten* by Jan Brett.			
Lowe, D.	*Wheels.*	Crystal Lake, Ill.: Rigby, 1988. Actual photographs match text about all kinds of wheels.	A
Feature: Relate to math unit on geometric shapes—circle.			
Raffi.	*Wheels on the Bus.*	New York: Crown, 1988. Text and illustrations relay traditional song.	A
Feature: Includes music; own verses may be added.			
Slater, T.	*The Bunny Hop.*	New York: Scholastic, 1992. Buddy Rabbit finally learns to dance.	A
Feature: Teach children the Bunny Hop.			
Ziefert, H.	*A Clean House for Mole and Mouse.*	New York: Scholastic, 1989. House cleaning makes mole hungry, but mouse won't let him eat in the clean house.	A
Feature: Relate to King's *Ants Love Picnics Too.*			
Beck, J.	*Pets.*	Crystal Lake, Ill.: Rigby, 1988. Little boy has all kinds of troubles with his pets. Will Mom let him get the dog he wants?	B
Feature: Strong rhyme helps with prediction.			
Blocksma, M.	*Apple Tree! Apple Tree!*	Chicago: Children's Press, 1983. Apple tree shares its fruit until worm leaves, but tree finds new friends in the spring.	B
Feature: Relate to Gordon's *Now I Know Trees.*			
Cartwright, P.	*The Wedding.*	Crystal Lake, Ill.: Rigby, 1988. Children decide to spend a rainy day having a wedding.	B
Feature: Discuss what can be done on a rainy day; relate to the rhyme "Rain, rain go away; Little Johnny wants to play."			

Author	Title	Information	Level
dePaola, T.	*The Knight and the Dragon.*	New York: G. P. Putman's Sons, 1980. Knight and Dragon go to the library to learn how to fight.	B
Feature: Discuss uses of the library.			
Johnson, C.	*The Blue Ribbon Puppies.*	New York: Harper & Row, 1958. Giving a blue ribbon to the "best" puppy results in all puppies coming in "first."	B
Feature: Good basis for discussion about what thing each child does especially well.			
Mahy, M.	*The Spider in the Shower.*	Crystal Lake, Ill.: Rigby, 1988. Rooster saves the day for his friends who are afraid of a spider in the shower.	B
Feature: Uses question mark and exclamation point.			
Obligado, L. (illustrator).	*Three Little Kittens.*	New York: Random House, 1974. Classic children's nursery rhyme of three naughty kittens.	B
Feature: Use for dramatization.			
Seuss, T.	*Mr. Brown Can Moo!*	New York: Random House, 1970. Mr. Brown can not only "moo," he makes all kinds of noises.	B
Feature: Very descriptive; uses onomatopoeia.			
Hoff, S.	*Wilfred the Lion.*	New York: G. P. Putman's Sons, 1970. A little boy who wants to be as brave as a lion turns into one!	C
Feature: Relate to Carle's *The Mixed-Up Chameleon.*			

Personal Additions:

Sample Lesson—Diphthongs

Note:

I would introduce only one sound made by diphthongs at a time. The lesson below discusses the "ow" sound made by the *ou* and *ow* diphthongs. I would introduce the "oy" sound made by *oy* (boy) and *oi* (oil), the "ew" sound made by *ew* (new) and *oo* (school), and the short "oo" sound made by *oo* as in *book* in different lessons, preferably separated by intervals of several weeks. Make the children aware of diphthongs, but do not drill either the term or the concept; this seems to be an area children learn once they have exposure to many words.

Book:

The Wheels on the Bus

Introduction:

Using the book, have children sing and dramatize the text.

Lesson:

"There are lots of words in this story where *o* and *u* or *o* and *w* come together to make an 'ow' sound. Let's say the first verse slowly; raise your hand if you hear a word that has an 'ow' sound in it."

Read: *The wheels on the bus go round and round,/Round and round, round and round./The wheels on the bus go round and round,/All through the town.*

"What words did we hear?" [round, town] Write the words on the board.

"In some words, vowels come together to make one different kind sound; something like the *th* digraph we talked about in the word *the*. The *t* doesn't say 't' and the *h* doesn't say 'h'; they work together to make a new sound of 'th.' Vowels can work together like that too. In the word *around*, the *o* and the *u* work together to make the 'ow' sound. In the word *town*, the *o* and the *w* work together to make the 'ow' sound. Let's think of words that rhyme with *round* and *town*." Write words under *round* or *town* so children can see spelling patterns; examples might be *sound, found, mound,* or *brown, clown, crown.*

Follow-up activity:

The only emphasis I would give to diphthongs is having the children go on an occasional "word hunt." Choose some appropriate books and ask the children to see how many "oi" (or some other diphthong) words they can find. Ask the children to read the sentence in which the word was found; discuss all the things in the sentence or in the picture that helped them know what the word might be. List the words on a designated chart to which the children can refer.

R-Controlled Vowels

When **r** follows a single vowel, it changes the sound that vowel would otherwise make.

Examples:

ar	*or*	*ir*	*er*	*ur*
car	for	girl	her	turn
dark	born	circus	after	church
yard	storm	bird	perch	hurt

Writing/Spelling Connection

The letter *r* controls a preceding vowel so much that children often think it is the *r* alone making the sound they hear. You will often see *girl* spelled *grl* or *bird* spelled *brd*. Reminding the students that every word (and, when they are ready, that every syllable) must have a vowel helps them realize that one of the vowels must accompany the *r*. Which vowel it is remains a mystery, especially because *ir, er,* and *ur* make the same sound in many words. Again, finding key words the children seem to recognize easily by sight and building word families around those key words seems the best way to teach the spelling patterns of the r-controlled vowels. In addition, point out to the children that many of the two-syllable words ending with an *r* sound that they read and write end with an *er* (*mother, father, brother, sister, water, over, letter, dinner, quarter, after . . .*).

Bibliographic Information and Annotations

Author	Title	Information	Level
Cowley, J.	*Don't You Laugh at Me.*	San Diego, Calif.: Wright Group, 1987. The hiccups save the day for animal friends that just can't stop laughing.	A
Feature: Frequent use of quotation marks.			
Hillman, J.	*When I Was Sick.*	Crystal Lake, Ill.: Rigby, 1989. A special letter cheers up a sick friend.	A
Feature: Use as basis for letter-writing activity.			
Kuchalla, S.	*Now I Know Bears.*	Mahwah, N.J.: Troll, 1982. Relates characteristics and habitat of bears.	A
Feature: Nonfiction; relate to Latham's and Sloan's *Why Do Polar Bears Like the Arctic?*			
Williams, R.	*Who's Hiding?*	Cypress, Calif.: Creative Teaching Press, 1994. Animals hide from predators.	A
Feature: Discuss the concept of food chains; relate to Cowley's *Spider, Spider.*			
Cowley, J.	*To Town.*	San Diego, Calif.: Wright Group, 1983. There are many fun ways to travel to town.	B
Feature: Relate to math graphing; graph favorite modes of transportation.			
Fowler, A.	*It Could Still Be a Bird.*	Chicago: Children's Press, 1990. Different birds and their characteristics are discussed in text and illustrated through beautiful photographs.	B
Feature: Relate to Fowler's *It Could Still Be a Fish* and Oppenheim's *Have You Seen Birds?*			
Gordon, S.	*What a Dog!*	Mahwah, N.J.: Troll, 1980. Taking Bernie for a walk results in more of an adventure than Billy had in mind.	B
Feature: Reinforces family names.			
Granowsky, A.	*The Panda.*	Cleveland, Ohio: Modern Curriculum Press, 1983. Explores the life and habits of the giant panda.	B
Feature: Nonfiction; relate to Allen's *Baby Panda at the Fair.*			
Granowsky, A., Tweedt, J., and Tweedt, C.	*Chicken Salad Soup.*	Cleveland, Ohio: Modern Curriculum Press, 1985. Recipe fed into a computer does not result in the expected chicken soup.	B
Feature: Write recipe for chicken soup; make it!			
Greydanus, R.	*Now I Know Horses.*	Mahwah, N.J.: Troll, 1983. Discusses characteristics of different horses.	B
Feature: Nonfiction; relate to Kuchalla's *Now I Know Bears.*			
King, S.	*Grandpa Snored.*	Crystal Lake, Ill.: Rigby, 1987. Nothing wakes up Grandpa until Grandma turns off the TV.	B
Feature: Uses onomatopoeia.			

Author	Title	Information	Level
Kraus, R.	*Whose Mouse Are You?*	New York: Scholastic, 1970. Lonely mouse is reunited with his family.	B
Feature: Reinforces family names.			
Krauss, R.	*The Carrot Seed.*	New York: Scholastic, 1945. A little boy's care of a seed pays off despite his family's lack of faith.	B
Feature: Relate to Titherington's *Pumpkin, Pumpkin.*			
Kuchalla, S.	*Now I Know Birds.*	Mahwah, N.J.: Troll, 1982. Discusses different kinds of birds, their characteristics and habitats.	B
Feature: Nonfiction; relate to Kuchalla's *Now I Know Bears*; compare format.			
Latham, R., and Sloan, P.	*The Bulldozer.*	Crystal Lake, Ill.: Rigby., 1985. Cumulative text relates basic steps in road construction.	B
Feature: Nonfiction; good for sequencing activity.			
Wandelmaier, R.	*Now I Know Stars.*	Mahwah, N.J.: Troll, 1985. Describes origin, sizes, and temperatures of stars.	B
Feature: Nonfiction; relate to concept of stars as "little twinkling lights."			
Crawford, T.	*A Bath for a Beagle.*	Mahwah, N.J.: Troll, 1970. Burton makes bath time quite an adventure.	C
Feature: Relate to Gordon's *What a Dog!*			
Robinson, E.	*A Rhinoceros? Preposterous!*	New York: DLM Teaching Resources, 1987. No one will believe a rhino is around, until he is found in the bedroom.	C
Feature: Strong rhyme supports reading more difficult words; uses question mark and exclamation point.			
Semple, C., and Tuer, J.	*Pancakes for Supper.*	Crystal Lake, Ill.: Rigby, 1988. Making pancakes for Grandpa and Grandma ends in a surprise for all.	C
Feature: Write recipe for pancakes; make them; relate to Granowsky's and Tweedts's *Chicken Salad Soup.*			

Personal Additions:

Sample Lesson—
R-Controlled Vowels

Note:

In the lesson below, the concept of the r-controlled vowel is referred to as "Bossy R." As with other metaphors or analogies, if you sense the children are more confused than helped by the descriptive language, simplify the explanation to "a strong *r*."

Book:

Don't You Laugh At Me

Introduction:

"This story always makes me laugh. Have any of you ever laughed so hard you got the hiccups?" Discuss.

"What animals were in this story?" [spider, bird, cat, dog, tiger, alligator] List characters on the board, placing those with an r-controlled vowel in one column. [spider, bird, tiger, alligator]

Lesson:

"When I read this list of words, I hear the sound of *r* in all of them." Read list, somewhat emphasizing the r-controlled sound.

"All these words have an *r* in them, and sometimes *r* can be kind of bossy. It likes to act like it is the only letter that makes the 'rrr' sound. But in *spider*, it is an *er* that makes that sound; in *bird,* it is an *ir* that makes that sound; in *tiger*, it is an *er* that makes that sound; and in *alligator*, it is an *or* that makes that sound. When you hear the sound of *r* in the middle or at the end of a word, it usually has a vowel that comes before it."

"Look at these words and let's see how bossy *r* can be." List *star, farm, corn, north, first, stir, herd, winner, curl,* and *fur.* Discuss how the vowels do not make the expected sound because the 'Bossy R' takes over.

"Some special words that I can think of that have that 'Bossy R' are *mother, father, sister,* and *brother.* Look for those when you are reading, or think about that "Bossy R" when you write about your family."

Follow-up activity:

R-controlled vowels, like diphthongs, become cemented after repeated opportunities to read and write the words. In the beginning, be happy that the children include *any* vowel with that r-controlled sound. Categorize words already seen in print, from books, or on cards, if only to further expose the children to the proper spellings. Pick words the children frequently meet in their reading and use in their writing and color code them on cards that can be easily categorized. For example, make words ending in *er* blue, words with *ir* green, words with *ur* red. Model thinking about r-controlled vowels by mentioning their occurrence to the children: "Oh, *hurt*; that's one of those words when *r* wants to pretend it's the only sound that is heard. But look, there's a *u* before it."

Soft and Hard G and C

When *g* or *c* is followed by an *i, e,* or *y,* it has a soft sound; when *g* or *c* is followed by an *a, o,* or *u,* or is the last letter of a word, it has a hard sound.

Examples:

Hard g	Soft g	Hard c	Soft c
gas	giraffe	cap	city
go	age	coat	dance
gum	gypsy	cut	fancy
bag		picnic	

Writing/Spelling Connection

Most alphabet books, when choosing only one sound for *g* and *c*, present the hard sound. I have always found that interesting, because saying the letters' names produces the soft sound. Yet children come to first grade usually saying "*g* is for goat" and "*c* is for cat." That's great; they're right. However, many of the words they will read and want to write do not have the hard sound for *g* and *c*. Rather than tell the children that those words are "exceptions," make them aware that the vowel following the *g* and *c* decides what sound it will make. The words *garage* and *circus* are great examples to illustrate that the *g* and *c* can make both sounds in one word because of the different vowels that follow the letter. Group *a, o,* and *u* together with examples of common hard *g* and *c* words; group *e, i,* and *y* together with examples of common soft *g* and *c* words. Display these charts so the students can use them as a reference.

Bibliographic Information and Annotations

Author	Title	Information	Level
Butler, A.	*On a Cold, Cold Day.*	Crystal Lake, Ill.: Rigby, 1984. Animals wear clothes to keep warm.	A
Feature: Emphasizes sound of *g*; rhyme helps with prediction.			
Cannard, E.	*Munching Mark.*	Crystal Lake, Ill.: Rigby, 1984. Marks munching habits lead to a toothache.	A
Feature: Emphasizes sound of *c*; relate to dental health unit.			
Cowley, J.	*Grumpy Elephant.*	San Diego, Calif.: Wright Group, 1982. A mishap among animal friends finally cheers up a grumpy elephant.	A
Feature: Emphasizes sound of *g*; use to discuss what might have made elephant grumpy.			
Cowley, J.	*I Am a Bookworm.*	San Diego, Calif.: Wright Group, 1986. A bookworm can devour many exciting things.	A
Feature: Emphasizes sound of *g*; relate to graphing in math; graph favorite types of books.			
Crews, D.	*Freight Train.*	New York: Scholastic, 1989. Colorful description of a freight train moving to its destination.	A
Feature: Nonfiction; emphasizes sound of *c*; good for sequencing events.			
McCracken, R., and M.	*What Is It?*	Winnipeg, Manitoba: Peguis, 1991. Book identifies common animals.	A
Feature: Nonfiction; emphasizes sound of *g*; use as a model for writing riddles.			
Nash, P.	*Rice.*	Cleveland, Ohio: Modern Curriculum Press, 1983. Relates the growing cycle and uses of rice.	A
Feature: Nonfiction; emphasizes sound of *c*; relate to Cowley's *The Pumpkin*.			
Urmston, K., and Evans, K.	*The Marching Band.*	New York: Kaeden, 1991. Many instruments make up a marching band.	A
Feature: Emphasizes sound of *c*; listen to tape of band music and try to identify instruments in the book.			
Van Allen, R.	*At the Zoo.*	Allen, Tex.: DLM Teaching Resources, 1985. Predictable verses tell about animals seen at the zoo.	A
Feature: Emphasizes sound of *g*; relate to Greydanus's *Animals at the Zoo*.			
Allen, C.	*More and More Clowns.*	Boston: Houghton Mifflin, All kinds of clowns come out of a circus car.	B
Feature: Emphasizes sound of *c*; uses comparatives *er* and *est*.			
Cowley, J.	*Greedy Cat.*	Wellington, New Zealand: School Publications of the Department of Education, 1983. Greedy cat snoops into the shopping bag once too often.	B
Feature: Emphasizes sound of *g*; relate to Buckley's *Greedy Gray Octopus*.			

Author	Title	Information	Level
Granowsky, A.	*The Dragon.*	Cleveland, Ohio: Modern Curriculum Press, 1983. Describes what people have thought about dragons.	B
Feature: Nonfiction; emphasizes sound of *g*; relate to Prelutsky's *The Dragons Are Singing Tonight.*			
McKissack, P. and F.	*Country Mouse and City Mouse.*	Chicago: Regensteiner, 1989. Classic tale ending with "there's no place like home."	B
Feature: Emphasizes sound of *c*; relate to Wilson's *Summer Camp.*			
Schorsch, K.	*Stone Soup.*	New York: Checkerboard Press, 1989. Traditional folk tale retold using rebus format.	B
Feature: Emphasizes sound of *g*; use as a model for writing class rebus stories.			
Fowler, A.	*Hearing Things.*	Chicago: Children's Press, 1991. Photographs enhance text, which discusses sense of hearing.	C
Feature: Nonfiction; emphasizes sound of *c* and *g*; relate to science unit on senses.			
Fowler, A.	*It's a Good Thing There Are Insects.*	Chicago: Children's Press, 1990. Describes characteristics of various insects and why they are important to the ecosystem.	C
Feature: Nonfiction; emphasizes sound of *c*; relate to Pallotta's *The Icky Bug Alphabet Book.*			
Gackenbach, D.	*Mag the Magnificent.*	New York: Clarion Books, 1985. Putting on an Indian costume begins a series of magical events.	C
Feature: Emphasizes sound of *g*.			
Granowsky, A.	*The Kangaroo.*	Cleveland, Ohio: Modern Curriculum Press, 1983. Describes characteristics and habits of the kangaroo.	C
Feature: Nonfiction; emphasizes sound of *g*; relate to Masters's *Kangaroo's Umbrella.*			
Kraus, R.	*How Spider Saved Easter.*	New York: Scholastic, 1988. Spider helps Ladybug win the first place trophy in the Easter Parade.	C
Feature: Emphasizes sound of *c*; use to discuss the real function of spiders.			
Marshall, J.	*Yummers!*	Boston: Houghton Mifflin, 1973. Emily can't understand why her walking for exercise results in her not feeling well.	C
Feature: Emphasizes sound of *c* and *g*; relate to Butler's *Tommy's Tummy Ache.*			
Sendak, M.	*Chicken Soup with Rice.*	New York: Scholastic, 1962. A verse for each month carries your imagination, and chicken soup, through a year.	C
Feature: Emphasizes sound of *c*; relate to months of the year; relate to Nash's nonfiction book, *Rice.*			

Personal Additions:

Sample Lesson— Hard and Soft G and C

Note:

This lesson discusses hard and soft *c*; a similar introductory lesson may be done with the sound of *g* using the words *grumpy* elephant and *giraffe* from Cowley's *Grumpy Elephant*.

Book:

Country Mouse and City Mouse

Introduction:

"Do you think Country Mouse will visit City Mouse again?" Discuss.

"I noticed something interesting about the title of our story. *Country* and *city* both begin with *c*. Does anyone else find that interesting?" See if anyone mentions the two different sounds of *c*; if not, direct their attention to it.

Lesson:

"Yes, the *c* in *country* makes a sound like *k*; we call that the hard sound of *c*. The *c* in *city* makes a sound like *s*; we call that the soft sound of *c*. There is a way we can tell whether *c* will sound like a *k* or like an *s*. I have a list of words on the board. One list is of hard *c* words; the other is of soft *c* words. Let's read the words." [*cat, cape, coat, cotton, curtain, cut,* and *cent, cereal, circle, cigar, cycle, cyclone*]

"Be word detectives and tell me what you notice about the hard *c* words?" Discuss; depending on children's responses, you may need to "give them a clue" and mention that "it has something to do with the vowel."

"What about the soft *c* words?" Discuss.

"So the vowels decide what sound the *c* will make. If an *a, o,* or *u* is after the *c*, the *c* will make a sound like *k,* or be a hard *c*. If an *i, e,* or *y* is after the *c*, the *c* will make a sound like *s,* or be a soft *c*."

"So why does Country Mouse's name start with a hard *c*?" [followed by *o*] "And why does City Mouse's name start with a soft *c*?" [followed by *i*]

"And what kind of *c* did we hear in the word *cat* that was in the story? Why?" [hard *c*; followed by an *a*]

State generalization:

"Sometimes when you are trying to figure out a word and you want to say just the first sound and read on, it may help you to know whether to say a hard or soft *c*. Remember, the vowel will let you know what to do."

Follow-up activity:

Include hard and soft *g* in this activity. Have pictures of objects that begin with hard and soft *c* and *g*. Children take turns rolling a die. If the number rolled is even, the child must find and name a picture that begins with soft *c* or *g*; if the number rolled is odd, the child must find and name a picture that begins with hard *c* or *g*. To extend this activity, have the words printed on the back of the card and ask the child to explain why the letter had the hard or soft sound. A variation is to use words instead of pictures, but make sure the child reads the word to avoid children just picking up a card because they saw a *gi* or a *ca*.

Word Ending—ing

This common English suffix may be added to base words to form nouns (a building), adjectives (the swimming team), or to express a different tense of a verb (is jumping).

Examples:

noun	adjective	verb
the bedding	sailing ship	running
his writing	shimmering lake	working
Mom's baking	teaching manual	laughing

Writing/Spelling Connection

Unlike some other suffixes, *ing* consistently says *ing*. It is usually an easy sound for the children to hear and to incorporate into their writing. Asking them "What three letters make that sound?" and having a reference chart that places common *ing* words beneath each picture will help the children become more aware of this phonetic element. When the students are ready, (introducing this too early will cause confusion and will inhibit the frequency and ease with which students will try to use the *ing* ending), they may be taught the various rules for adding the *ing* suffix.

For words ending in a silent *e*, drop the *e* and add *ing* (skating; liking; hoping).

For short-vowel words ending in a single consonant, double the final consonant and then add *ing* (hopping; skipping; running).

For short-vowel words ending in more than one consonant, do not double the final consonant before adding *ing* (jumping; laughing; hunting).

For long-vowel words, do not double the final consonant before adding *ing* (bleeding; reading; raining).

Bibliographic Information and Annotations

Author	Title	Information	Level
Cowley, J.	*The Jigaree.*	San Diego, Calif.: Wright Group, 1989. A space traveler meets a Jigaree who follows him everywhere, including home.	A
Feature: Excellent book for introducing *ing* concept.			
Lawrence, L.	*Fly, Fly Witchy.*	Crystal Lake, Ill.: Rigby, 1990. Halloween characters join the witch for trick-or-treating fun.	A
Feature: Can be sung to the tune "She'll be coming around the mountain"; good for dramatization.			
Martin, B., and Archambault, J.	*Here Are My Hands.*	New York: Henry Holt, 1985. Various activities are related to different body parts.	A
Feature: Use as basis for discussion or writing about what else hands or feet can do.			
Martin, B.	*Polar Bear, Polar Bear, What Do You Hear?*	New York: Henry Holt, 1991. Rhythmic pattern presents animal sounds at the zoo.	A
Feature: Good for dramatization; relate to Martin's *Brown Bear, Brown Bear, What Do You See?*			
McCracken, R. and M.	*What Can You Hear?*	Winnipeg, Manitoba: Peguis, Ltd., 1991. Repeating pattern "I can hear . . ." presents various sounds.	A
Feature: Easy to use as a model for a class book; relate to Martin's *Polar Bear, Polar Bear, What Do You Hear?*			
Barchas, S.	*I Was Walking Down the Road.*	New York: Scholastic, 1975. A girl collects several pets only to set them free.	B
Feature: Strong rhyme helps with prediction of text.			
Baum, A. and J.	*One Bright Monday Morning.*	New York: Silver Burdett & Ginn, 1989. Cumulative pattern presents days of the week and numbers one through seven as person counts objects seen on the way to school.	B
Feature: Simple geometric shapes used in pictures can be used to reinforce concepts of shape and color.			
Hutchins, P.	*The Surprise Party.*	New York: Aladdin Books, 1991. The news of rabbit's surprise party gets all mixed up as it travels from one friend to another.	B
Feature: Practice listening skills by playing "Telephone": one child whispers a message to another and last child repeats the message as it came to him or her.			
Jorgensen, G.	*Crocodile Beat.*	Crystal Lake, Ill.: Rigby, 1988. Rhythmic text tells of jungle animals joining in a celebration until a crocodile comes to spoil the fun.	B
Feature: Accompanying tape available; uses onomatopoeia.			
Semple, C., and Tuer, J.	*Lilly-Lolly Little Legs.*	Crystal Lake, Ill.: Rigby, 1988. Lilly-Lolly can't join her friends in play because she is always busy doing something else, until they ask her to be the top of a pyramid.	B
Feature: Uses exclamation point and question mark.			

Author	Title	Information	Level
Allen, C.	*Beautiful Breezy Blue and White Day.*	Allen, Tex.: DLM Teaching Resources, 1989. Clouds take on shapes of creatures doing various things.	C
Feature: Rhyme helps with prediction; good basis for art lesson using torn paper shapes; relate to Shaw's *It Looked Like Spilt Milk.*			
Allen, T.	*Baby Panda at the Fair.*	Allen, Tex.: DLM Teaching Resources, 1986. Baby Panda causes "pandemonium" when he gets lost at the fair.	C
Feature: Rhyme helps with prediction; good book for modeling use of prior knowledge (discuss places where Panda could be).			
Carle, E.	*The Very Quiet Cricket.*	New York: Philomel Books, 1990. Young cricket meets various insects and repeatedly cannot chirp until he meets just the right friend.	C
Feature: Cricket-like sound is actually heard as reader opens the last page! Good book to model alternatives to using the word *said*.			
Kimmel, E.	*Anansi and the Moss-Covered Rock.*	New York: Scholastic, 1988. Anansi the Spider tricks all his friends until he meets the clever Little Bush Deer.	C
Feature: Good inspiration for oral language, discuss what children think was magical about the rock, or what made everyone faint?			
Oppenheim, J.	*Have You Seen Birds?*	New York: Scholastic, 1986. Text discusses different birds in various habitats and activities.	C
Feature: Unique illustrations provide model for art experience with clay.			
Robinson, E.	*The Dinosaur Ball.*	Allen, Tex.: DLM Teaching Resources, 1987. Cumulative story tells of common dinosaurs who accept an invitation to a ball until they discover that one of the guests is a hungry Tyrannosaurus Rex!	C
Feature: Pronunciation guide for dinosaur names is included on the last page; relate to Marzollo's *I'm Tyrannosaurus.*			
Sendak, M.	*Chicken Soup with Rice.*	New York: Scholastic, 1962. Activities describe each month of the year, all ending with repetitious stanza about chicken soup.	C
Feature: Relate to studying months of the year.			
Wood, A.	*The Napping House.*	New York: Harcourt Brace Jovanovich, 1984. Cumulative pattern tells of a pileup on a cozy bed until a flea happens by!	C
Feature: Models cumulative writing pattern; relate to McClintock's *A Fly Went By.*			

Personal Additions:

Sample Lesson— Word Ending ing

Note:

Distinguish between *ing* as part of a base word (*king*, *string*) and its use as a word ending. Show the students that if *ing* is removed from *king* or *string* there is no longer a word; if it is removed from *jumping* or *building*, there is still a word—the base word (some teachers prefer to call it a root word).

Book:

The Jigaree

Introduction:

Discuss what it would be like to travel on a different planet. What might you see? What would be the same as on Earth?

"What were some things the Jigaree and the space traveler did together?" As children respond, list the *ing* words on the board.

"Are there any similarities among the words on the board?" [*ing* ending]

Lesson:

Discuss the idea of a word ending; show that by removing the *ing* we are left with a base or root word.

"What are some things you like to do?" [reading, walking, playing] As children respond, write the *ing* word on a chart labeled "ING WORDS." Display the chart so it can be used as a reference.

"Now, let's look in our book again and count how many *ing* words are in this story."

State generalization:

Remind the children that knowing *ing* can help them with words they need to read and with words they may wish to write. Repeat the sound *ing* makes and ask what three letters make that sound.

Follow-up activity:

Make a class book, or individual ones, illustrating and labeling actions the students can do. For example, "Here we are walking. Here we are reading. Here we are sleeping, . . . eating, playing, dancing."

Word Ending—ed

This common English suffix may be added to base words to form adjectives from nouns (bearded man) or to express the past tense of verbs (walked).

Examples:

adjectives	verbs—ed	verbs—d	verbs—t
learned	landed	lived	bumped
aged	painted	rained	dressed
skinned	ended	spelled	kissed

Writing/Spelling Connection

The *ed* suffix is not as easy to learn as the *ing* suffix because it can make three different sounds. For a long time children will spell words like *jumped* with a *t* at the end; not until they realize visual spelling can override sound do they consistently add *ed* endings correctly. Once this suffix is introduced, display a three-sectioned chart labeled "*ed as ed*," "*ed as d*," and "*ed as t*." Laminate the chart so it can be reused, or corrected if necessary. As children find words in their reading that have an *ed* ending (not words that end with *ed*, like *bed*), allow them to write the word under the correct column. This activity will increase their awareness of *ed* endings and the different sounds they can make. Assure the children that they almost always will know what sound the *ed* ending makes because they know how to say the words; reinforce that knowing how language sounds is a great help in learning how to read and write.

Bibliographic Information and Annotations

Author	Title	Information	Level
Buffington, V.	*Who Cried for Pie?*	Mahwah, N.J.: Troll, 1970. Guess who gets the cherry pie the family made?	A
Feature: Contains all three sounds of *ed*; uses question mark.			
Cowley, J.	*Come for a Swim!*	San Diego, Calif.: Wright Group, 1987. Dad and the children find a way to get Mom to join them for a swim.	A
Feature: Uses quotation marks.			
Cowley, J.	*Mr. Grump.*	San Diego, Calif.: Wright Group, 1987. A kiss from Mrs. Grump changes everything.	A
Feature: Relate to Cowley's *Grumpy Elephant.*			
Cowley, J.	*The Pumpkin.*	San Diego, Calif.: Wright Group, 1982. Each family member helped make a pumpkin treat possible.	A
Feature: Relate to graphing in math; graph favorite way to eat pumpkin, or apples. . . .			
Cowley, J.	*The Seed.*	San Diego, Calif.: Wright Group, 1987. A forgotten seed yields a hefty surprise.	A
Feature: Emphasizes all three sounds of *ed*; relate to Lobel's "The Garden" in *Frog and Toad Together.*			
Chase, E., and Reid, B.	*The New Baby Calf.*	New York: Scholastic, 1984. Story follows baby calf as it grows up.	B
Feature: Relate to Melser's *Three Little Ducks.*			
Christelow, W.	*Five Little Monkeys Jumping on the Bed.*	New York: Clarion Books, 1989. Surprise ending to this classic rhyme will delight the reader.	B
Feature: Print variation indicates voice volume.			
Cowley, J.	*Mrs. Wishy Washy.*	San Diego, Calif.: Wright Group, 1980. Stubborn animals just can't resist that lovely mud!	B
Feature: Relate to Cowley's *Wishy Washy Day.*			
Guarino, D.	*Is Your Mama a Llama?*	New York: Scholastic, 1989. Riddles describe animal features. Illustrated by Steven Kellogg.	B
Feature: Good for prediction; model for writing riddle format.			
Aardema, V.	*Bringing the Rain to Kapiti Plain.*	New York: Dial Books for Young Readers, 1981. Cumulative verse about the rain that comes to the plains of Kenya, Africa.	C
Feature: Locate Kenya on map; relate to Musgrove's *Ashanti to Zulu: African Traditions.*			
Carle, E.	*Rooster's Off to See the World.*	Saxonville, Mass.: Picture Book Studio, 1972. Rooster's ill-prepared trip results in homesickness and loss of traveling companions.	C
Feature: Relate to math addition and subtraction units.			

Author	Title	Information	Level
Cole, J.	*Boney-Legs.*	New York: Scholastic, 1983. Kind girl outsmarts mean witch.	C
Feature: Emphasizes all three sounds of *ed*; relate to Hansel and Gretel.			
Drew, D.	*Caterpillar Diary.*	Crystal Lake, Ill.: Rigby, 1987. Beautiful photographs chronicle the fifteen-week life cycle of the moth.	C
Feature: Nonfiction; relate to Bailey's *Butterflies and Moths*.			
Freeman, D.	*Corduroy.*	New York: Scholastic, 1968. A lovable teddy bear finds the friend he always wanted.	C
Feature: Emphasizes all three sounds of *ed*.			
Galdone, P.	*The Little Red Hen.*	New York: Clarion Books, 1973. Traditional fairy tale.	C
Feature: Emphasizes all three sounds of *ed*.			
Hall, D.	*Ox-Cart Man.*	New York: Scholastic, 1979. Relates cycles of life and livelihood of a farm family.	C
Feature: Good book for sequencing.			
Hutchins, P.	*Good Night, Owl.*	Boston: Houghton Mifflin, 1989. Daytime friends keep owl awake, but he seeks his revenge that night.	C
Feature: Uses onomatopoeia; good for dramatization.			
Kachenmeister, C.	*On Monday When It Rained.*	Boston: Houghton Mifflin, 1989. Each day of the week brings a new event and a different feeling.	C
Feature: Emphasizes all three sounds of *ed*; photographs are model for fun class book activity.			
Parkes, B., and Smith, J.	*The Enormous Watermelon.*	Crystal Lake, Ill.: Rigby, 1986. Mother Hubbard asks nursery rhyme characters to help her pull up an enormous watermelon.	C
Feature: Relate to McKibben's *The Big Enormous Turnip*.			
Sendak, M.	*Where the Wild Things Are.*	New York: Harper & Row, 1963. Sent to bed without supper, Max becomes king of the Wild Things.	C
Feature: Relate to Mayer's *There's a Nightmare in My Closet*.			
Slobodkina, E.	*Caps for Sale.*	New York: Harper & Row, 1987. Peddler runs into real monkey business when trying to sell his caps.	C
Feature: Emphasizes all three sounds of *ed*; reinforces color words; good for dramatization.			

Personal Additions:

Sample Lesson—
Word Ending—ed

Note:

This lesson assumes the children have already been introduced to the idea of word endings and are familiar with using *ing*.

Book:

Where the Wild Things Are

Introduction:

"One of my favorite parts of this story is when Max decides to leave the Wild Things. I'm going to read those two pages again; listen for all the things Max and the Wild Things do." Read pages twelve and thirteen.

"Who can tell me something Max or the Wild Things did?" [cried, stepped, waved, gnashed, rolled, growled, showed, roared] As children respond, list words on the board, lining up the *ed* endings.

"What do you notice about all these words?" [all end with *ed*]

Lesson:

"Yes, *ed* is another word ending, but *ed* is different from *ing*. The *ing* word ending always makes the same sound. The *ed* word ending can make more than one sound. Let's read the words again and listen for the sound we hear at the end." Read and discuss.

"When you meet words with *ed* endings, you will know what the *ed* says because you already know how to say the word. For example, you know that we do not say 'I jump -ed (saying *ed* as Ed) the rope'; we say 'I jumped (saying *ed* as t) the rope.' You can use all the wonderful things you know about speaking to help you when you read words with *ed* endings."

Explain three-column chart labeled "ED ENDINGS." Invite children to write words they find under the appropriate column: *ed as ed*; *ed as d*; or *ed as t*. You might want to begin the list by adding the *ed* words from *Where the Wild Things Are*.

Follow-up activity:

On individual cards, write words that children would commonly see with *ed* endings. Make the card so the *ed* ending could be folded back. Children can practice reading the base word, then extending the end of the card and reading the word with the *ed* ending. Require that they either define the word or use it in a sentence. Occasionally, ask children to go for a word hunt, looking for words with *ed* endings. Be sure they do not choose words in which the *ed* is part of the base word.

PART 2
HIGH-FREQUENCY WORDS

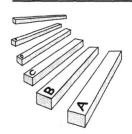

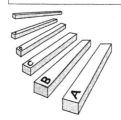

Chapter 3

Core Words

The first twenty-five most frequently used words make up about one-third of all printed material (Lawson et al. 1992). The importance of children building a basic sight vocabulary (words they readily recognize and understand) cannot be overstated. Readers who must labor over every word in the text cannot focus their attention on the meaning of the message. Nor can they use strategies, such as reading on for further clues, if the very next word, and the one after that, and the one after that are also unknown words. Writers who must labor through every word surely do not express the quantity of wonderful ideas they might otherwise share.

Certain basic words seem to provide the framework for the language itself. Several researchers have each tabulated lists of high-utility words, and their results are remarkably similar (Sitton 1990). A basic core of words appears repeatedly in the texts we read and the messages we write. (See appendixes B, C, and D.) Instant recognition of these words frees a reader to more actively engage in the problem-solving processes of reading and writing. These anchor words not only make comprehension and fluency easier to achieve, but also provide a source of growing self-confidence and act as checkpoints for readers and writers working with printed language.

The best way for children to learn high-frequency words is to continually see them in print and to use them frequently in their writing. By the fact that they *are* high-frequency words, children cannot help but come across them often in the stories they are reading; they cannot help but write them in the messages they want to put into print. So, sustained periods of reading and writing are highly recommended for high-frequency word acquisition.

In addition, certain activities can enhance and strengthen word recognition skills. As with phonics lessons, they should be done within the context of authentic reading and writing, and they should remain enjoyable and nonthreatening. Balance having fun with words in isolation and with meeting them in meaningful reading and writing situations. Children have a natural desire to learn, and learning about words should be exciting. The following activities are just samples of what can be done to increase awareness of high-frequency words.

Word a week. Beginning with the second week of school, concentrate on one high-frequency word a week. As the children's literacy experiences increase, you may be able to do two a week, or focus on a "family," like *is, it, in, if.* Begin with the most frequently written word: *the.* Talk about how it looks; count how many times it appears on a page in the book you have just read; practice writing it with tall, skinny letters and with short, fat letters; some teachers have the children decorate it with glitter. Put it on a poster that says "I'm Number One" and leave it up all year. Once you feel the children have had sufficient exposure to the word, and that will vary among students, hold them accountable for writing it correctly. Writing can be used to reinforce reading here, for the more the children make these words their own in their writing, the more automatically they will recognize them in the print of others. The expectation that "now that you know that word you will write it correctly" is one of the most significant factors in the students' achievement in both reading and writing.

After the word *the,* continue with the list in order of frequency, varying the activities. One time, students might "paint" the word on the board with water and watch it disappear; or they might trace it on a friend's back. The words should always be posted on a reference chart for the children. Some teachers post them individually on the ceiling. The students know where to look, and they know those are the words they are expected to use correctly. Remain encouraging, but offer support only to the degree the students need it. Prompts should become general: "Oh, that's one of the words we have talked about quite a bit; see if you can find it on the chart"; or "That's a word you know; think about it for a moment." Most first-grade students will be able to identify and correctly write the first twenty-five to forty high-frequency words by the end of the year; reading sight vocabulary will be even higher.

Table label. This ongoing activity exposes children to high-frequency words in a fun, casual way. Choose two or three different high-frequency words to tape to the middle of each table. When calling children to line up for something say: "If you are sitting at the table with the word 'the' (or 'and,' 'it,' 'was') your table may line up." Allow children to help each other. They are not being tested; rather, it is an opportunity for all children to look for the words in question. After a week or so, switch the words to different tables. Once the students seem to recognize all the words quickly, replace them with a new set. If your classroom has individual student desks, choose a high-frequency word for an entire row or one desk in each row; that way, students can still work cooperatively, Do not introduce too many high frequency words at one time.

Daily message. Writing a daily message to the children is a powerful tool. Begin with highly predictable messages. For example, "Today is Monday. We will go to the library. You are special." "Today is Tuesday. We will go to the computer lab. I like you." Once children become familiar with the routine, you can embellish the message so it is more challenging, but always keep it at a level where the students will feel successful. Again, you are giving the children an opportunity to play with words, not testing them to see who remembers what. Have children look for a certain word; ask one child to circle it in the message. Once the word is established, omit a letter and ask the children to supply it. "Today is Friday. W- will go to music. Y-- have been so good this week."

Concentration. Based on the popular television show, write each known high frequency word on two flash cards. Cards are turned blank side up, mixed, and arranged in rows. Children take turns turning two cards over, trying to make a pair. When a pair is matched, the player must read the word. If the word is correctly identified, the player gets to keep both cards. The player with the most cards at the end of the game wins.

Total recall. Use a deck of cards that is made of high-frequency words. Each word must appear on two cards. Cards are shuffled and dealt evenly between two children. Each player turns over a card at the same time. If the cards match, the child who correctly identifies the word first gets to keep both cards. The game ends when all the cards are matched; the player with the most cards wins.

Word jumbles. (This activity may be too frustrating for children who have trouble seeing words in left-to-right sequence. Monitor its use to avoid feelings of failure.) Prepare a set of cards with high-frequency words scrambled. Laminate the cards so they can be reused. Allow children to write the word with washable marker in its correct sequence beneath the jumbled letters. You may wish to numerically code each card so the children can independently check their responses with an answer sheet.

As stated earlier, the best way for children to learn high-frequency words is to see them often in print. The remainder of this chapter presents high-frequency words in alphabetical order. The first twenty-five most frequently used words are designated with an asterisk (*). Following each word are books in which that word occurs several times. These books can be used to reinforce a word being studied for the week or to review words already learned. Rarely should the main lesson of the book be the high-frequency word; the word will be strengthened as the book is used to teach broader strategies for reading. Encouraging students to write something about the story should provide an opportunity for the high-frequency word to be used in writing too.

As with the books selected for part 1 of this resource, the following books are not the only ones in which the given high-frequency words appear often. Teachers are encouraged to add personal favorites as they find literature they enjoy using with their students. The books selected below are ones commonly used in early intervention programs. Most books are identified by the series of which they are a part. The *Storybox Series* and the *Sunshine Series* are both publications of The Wright Group; *Literacy 2000* is published by Rigby; *Tiger Cub Books* are from Peguis, Inc.; *Troll* indicates publications from Troll Associates; and *DLM* denotes books from DLM Teaching Resources. The complete addresses for these publishers, and others frequently mentioned, may be found in appendix F.

Because of the number of words and volume of books, this bibliography is not annotated. The bibliographic information follows this format: Title of book; author's last name if selection is a trade book; individual publisher or name of series and publisher; suggested reading level; number of running words with the title counted once. The final item is included to help teachers who wish to take running records of students reading these books. For a detailed explanation of running records as a diagnostic, prescriptive, and evaluative tool refer to Marie Clay's publication, *The Early Detection of Reading Difficulties* (1979), or her more recent work, *An Observation Survey of Early Literacy Achievement* (1993). Rigby also offers two excellent videos by Leanna Traill in its 1995 catalog: *Learning Running Records* and *Using Running Records*.

Title (Author)	Series/Publisher	Level	Number of Words
a*			
Huggles' Breakfast	Sunshine/Wright Group	A	16
The Party	Storybox/Wright Group	A	16
A Toybox	Literacy 2000/Rigby	A	22
A Zoo	Literacy 2000/Rigby	A	16
What Are You?	Literacy 2000/Rigby	A	30
The Ghost	Storybox/Wright Group	A	28
Teeny Tiny Tina	Literacy 2000/Rigby	A	34
after			
No, No	Storybox/Wright Group	A	93
Two Little Dogs	Storybox/Wright Group	A	74
again			
Should You Ever?	Tiger Cub/Peguis	A	75
alike			
Muffy and Fluffy	Troll	B	159
all			
The Pumpkin	Storybox/Wright Group	A	58
Horace	Storybox/Wright Group	A	57
Wheels on the Bus (Raffi)	Crown	A	228
To Town	Storybox/Wright Group	B	147
along			
Along Comes Jake	Sunshine/Wright Group	A	89
The Night Train	Storybox/Wright Group	A	74
Grumpy Elephant	Storybox/Wright Group	A	103
Freddie the Frog	Troll	B	145
am			
What Are You?	Literacy 2000/Rigby	A	30

Title (Author)	Series/Publisher	Level	Number of Words
am *(cont.)*			
Major Jump	Sunshine/Wright Group	A	24
I Am Frightened	Storybox/Wright Group	A	44
Who's Going to Lick the Bowl	Storybox/Wright Group	A	24
The Haunted House	Storybox/Wright Group	A	80
an			
Huggles Can Juggle	Sunshine/Wright Group	A	18
Hungry Horse	Literacy 2000/Rigby	A	35
Elephant in Trouble	Troll	B	101
Who Will Be My Mother?	Storybox/Wright Group	B	160
I Know an Old Lady (Bonne)	Rand McNally	B	422
There Was an Old Lady	Child's Play (International)	C	189
and*			
Teeny Tiny Tina	Literacy 2000/Rigby	A	34
Tommy's Tummy Ache	Literacy 2000/Rigby	A	23
Painting	Storybox/Wright Group	A	25
Round and Round	Storybox/Wright Group	A	38
The Bicycle	Storybox/Wright Group	A	31
Houses	Storybox/Wright Group	A	61
No, No	StoryboxWright Group	A	93
Mrs. Wishy Washy	Storybox/Wright Group	B	105
Goodnight Moon (Brown)	Harper & Row	B	138
animals			
Animals at the Zoo	Troll	B	158
another			
Mother, Mother, I Want Another (Poluskin)	Crown	C	232

Title (Author)	Series/Publisher	Level	Number of Words
answer			
The Very Busy Spider (Carle)	Philomel Books	B	273
The Very Quiet Cricket (Carle)	Philomel Books	C	324
anyone			
The Maligned Mosquito	DLM	C	447
are*			
Where Are They Going?	Storybox/Wright Group	A	46
Buzzing Flies	Sunshine/Wright Group	A	47
Uncle Buncle's House	Sunshine/Wright Group	A	59
Danger	Storybox/Wright Group	A	68
Rum-tum-tum	Storybox/Wright Group	A	65
Mud Pies	Troll	B	157
Here Are My Hands (Martin, Jr.)	Henry Holt	B	100
The Penguins Come to Dinner	DLM	C	576
around			
Buzzing Flies	Sunshine/Wright Group	A	47
Wheels on the Bus (Raffi)	Crown	A	228
Rosie's Walk (Hutchins)	Collier Books	A	34
as*			
A Hug Is Warm	Sunshine/Wright Group	A	64
All Join In	Literacy 2000/Rigby	A	41
at*			
At the Zoo	DLM	A	153
Dizzy Lizzy	Literacy 2000/Rigby	B	37
More and More Clowns	DLM	B	253
away			
When Itchy Witchy Sneezes	Sunshine/Wright Group	A	43

Title (Author)	Series/Publisher	Level	Number of Words
away *(cont.)*			
Oh, Jump in a Sack	Storybox/Wright Group	A	130
Umbrella Parade	Troll	B	158
Come and Have Fun (Hurd)	Harper & Row	C	436
baby			
Don't Wake the Baby	Literacy 2000/Rigby	A	27
Baby's Birthday	Literacy 2000/Rigby	A	53
Baby Panda at the Fair	DLM	C	164
back			
Shoo!	Sunshine/Wright Group	A	38
The Red Rose	Storybox/Wright Group	A	129
Oh, Jump in a Sack	Storybox/Wright Group	A	130
Down by the Bay (Raffi)	Crown	B	248
be*			
Who Will Be My Mother?	Storybox/Wright Group	B	160
best			
Red Is Best (Stinson)	Firefly Books	C	312
big			
Big and Little	Sunshine/Wright Group	A	35
Blue Sea (Kalan)	Greenwillow Books	A	74
The Haunted House	Storybox/Wright Group	A	80
Too Big for Me	Storybox/Wright Group	A	77
Little Danny Dinosaur	Troll	B	198
Animals at the Zoo	Troll	B	158
To Town	Storybox/Wright Group	B	147
The Big Brown Teddy Bear	DLM	C	283
At the Carnival	DLM	C	376

Title (Author)	Series/Publisher	Level	Number of Words
bigger			
Blue Sea (Kalan)	Greenwillow Books	A	74
I'm Bigger Than You	Sunshine/Wright Group	A	52
Three Billy Goats Gruff	Scholastic	C	399
biggest			
Blue Sea (Kalan)	Greenwillow Books	A	74
blew			
Bubble Gum in the Sky	Troll	B	139
blows			
When Itchy Witchy Sneezes	Sunshine/Wright Group	A	43
box			
Jack-in-the-Box	Literacy 2000/Rigby	A	38
brought			
Drummer Hoff (Emberley)	Simon & Schuster	C	173
but			
Stop!	Storybox/Wright Group	A	55
The Seed	Sunshine/Wright Group	A	53
Green Eyes	Literacy 2000/Rigby	B	113
Scruffy Messed It Up	Literacy 2000/Rigby	B	109
If I Were a Fish	DLM	B	218
A Dream in a Wishing Well	DLM	B	399
Just for You (Mayer)	Golden Book	B	163
Mongon	DLM	C	279
The Penguins Come to Dinner	DLM	C	576
by			
Down by the Bay (Raffi)	Crown	B	248
called			
Shoo!	Sunshine/Wright Group	A	38

Title (Author)	Series/Publisher	Level	Number of Words

called *(cont.)*			
The Pet Parade	Literacy 2000/Rigby	A	33
In My Room	Literacy 2000/Rigby	A	49
Freddie the Frog	Troll	B	145
The Carrot Seed (Krauss)	Scholastic	B	104
The Doorbell Rang (Hutchins)	Scholastic	C	283
The Dinosaur Ball	DLM	C	294
can			
The Marching Band	Kaeden	A	38
Looking for Halloween	Kaeden	A	52
Plop!	Storybox/Wright Group	A	32
What Can You See?	Tiger Cub/Peguis	A	73
I Can Jump	Sunshine/Wright Group	A	43
The Monsters' Party	Storybox/Wright Group	A	95
Shark in a Sack	Sunshine/Wright Group	A	69
I Love Ladybugs	DLM	A	143
I Can Spell Dinosaur	DLM	A	152
What Can You Do?	Tiger Cub/Peguis	A	61
What Can You Hear?	Tiger Cub/Peguis	A	84
The Jigaree	Storybox/Wright Group	B	130
A Dream in a Wishing Well	DLM	B	399
Let's Get a Pet	Troll	B	148
Watch Your Step, Mr. Rabbit (Scarry)	Random House	B	98
Why Can't I Fly? (Gelman)	Scholastic	C	353
cannot			
Five Little Kittens	Troll	A	138
Freddie the Frog	Troll	B	145

Title (Author)	Series/Publisher	Level	Number of Words
can't			
I Can Jump	Sunshine/Wright Group	A	43
The Monsters' Party	Storybox/Wright Group	A	95
The Farm Concert	Storybox/Wright Group	A	77
I Can Spell Dinosaur	DLM	A	152
Horace	Storybox/Wright Group	A	57
Don't You Laugh at Me	Sunshine/Wright Group	A	175
Come On Up!	Troll	A	136
Who Will Be My Mother?	Storybox/Wright Group	B	160
A Dream in a Wishing Well	DLM	B	399
Lilly-Lolly Little Legs	Literacy 2000/Rigby	B	133
card			
Happy Birthday	Literacy 2000/Rigby	A	35
catch			
Dan, the Flying Man	Storybox/Wright Group	A	64
Too Big for Me	Storybox/Wright Group	A	77
caught			
What Did Kim Catch?	Literacy 2000/Rigby	B	48
I Was Walking Down the Road (Barchas)	Scholastic	B	305
chased			
Buffy	Literacy 2000/Rigby	A	33
come			
Come With Me	Storybox/Wright Group	A	28
Spider, Spider	Sunshine/Wright Group	A	72
No, No	Storybox/Wright Group	A	93
Horace	Storybox/Wright Group	A	57
Come On Up	Troll	A	136

Title (Author)	Series/Publisher	Level	Number of Words
come *(cont.)*			
Oh, Jump in a Sack	Storybox/Wright Group	A	130
More and More Clowns	DLM	B	253
Come and Have Fun (Hurd)	Harper & Row	C	436
The Penguins Come to Dinner	DLM	C	576
The Big Enormous Turnip	LINK	C	452
comes			
The Storm	Storybox/Wright Group	A	31
Along Comes Jake	Sunshine/Wright Group	A	89
Umbrella Parade	Troll	B	158
coming			
Come for a Swim	Storybox/Wright Group	A	134
Pancakes for Supper	Literacy 2000/Rigby	B	99
Noisy Neighbors	Troll	C	428
could/couldn't			
Leo the Late Bloomer (Kraus)	Windmill Books	C	168
The Big Enormous Turnip	LINK	C	452
daddy			
Lost	Storybox/Wright Group	A	39
Just Like Daddy (Asch)	Scholastic	B	96
did/didn't			
The Seed	Sunshine/Wright Group	A	53
The Very Busy Spider (Carle)	Philomel Books	B	273
Flying High	DLM	C	318
do			
Who Likes Ice Cream?	Storybox/Wright Group	A	95
Up in a Tree	Sunshine/Wright Group	A	51

Title (Author)	Series/Publisher	Level	Number of Words
do *(cont.)*			
Brown Bear, Brown Bear, What Do You See? (Martin, Jr.)	Holt, Rinehart & Winston	A	201
Where Do You Live?	Tiger Cub/Peguis	A	145
Polar Bear, Polar Bear, What Do You Hear? (Martin, Jr.)	Henry Holt	A	208
What Do You Do?	Tiger Cub/Peguis	A	162
What Do You Have?	Tiger Cub/Peguis	A	179
Animals at the Zoo	Troll	B	158
doesn't			
There's a Dragon in My Wagon (Nelson)	Modern Curriculum Press	B	77
The Maligned Mosquito	DLM	C	447
don't			
Lost	Storybox/Wright Group	A	39
Don't Wake the Baby	Literacy 2000/Rigby	A	27
Don't You Laugh at Me	Sunshine/Wright Group	A	175
I Know an Old Lady (Bonne)	Rand McNally	B	422
Mongon	DLM	C	279
There Was an Old Lady	Child's Play (International)	C	189
down			
Down to Town	Sunshine/Wright Group	A	29
I Can Fly	Sunshine/Wright Group	A	24
Flying	Storybox/Wright Group	A	27
Down by the Bay (Raffi)	Crown	B	248
I Was Walking Down the Street (Barchas)	Scholastic	B	305
enough			
Surprise Cake	Literacy 2000/Rigby	A	32

Title (Author)	Series/Publisher	Level	Number of Words
enough *(cont.)*			
The Grouchy Ladybug (Carle)	Harper & Row	C	822
ever			
Should You Ever?	Tiger Cub/Peguis	A	75
everyone			
One Light, One Sun (Raffi)	Crown	B	65
The Maligned Mosquito	DLM	C	447
everything			
Playground Fun	Troll	B	177
everywhere			
The Jigaree	Storybox/Wright Group	B	130
Cookie's Week (Ward)	Scholastic	B	85
At the Carnival	DLM	C	376
Baby Panda at the Fair	DLM	C	164
fell			
Five Little Monkeys Jumping on the Bed (Christelow)	Clarion Books	B	207
find			
Looking for Halloween	Kaeden	A	52
fix			
What a Mess!	Storybox/Wright Group	A	56
flew			
Bubble Gum in the Sky	Troll	B	139
fly			
Why Can't I Fly? (Gelman)	Scholastic	C	353
for*			
Sharing	Literacy 2000/Rigby	A	25
Look for Me	Storybox/Wright Group	A	74

Title (Author)	Series/Publisher	Level	Number of Words
colspan for* (cont.)
Wake Up, Mom	Sunshine/Wright Group	A	94
Danger	Storybox/Wright Group	A	68
Good for You	Sunshine/Wright Group	A	47
What's for Lunch?	Storybox/Wright Group	A	39
Too Big for Me	Storybox/Wright Group	A	77
In My Bed	Literacy 2000/Rigby	A	60
Here Are My Hands, (Martin, Jr.)	Henry Holt	B	100
Down by the Bay (Raffi)	Crown	B	248
Just for You (Mayer)	Golden Book	B	163
colspan forgot
Goodbye, Lucy	Sunshine/Wright Group	A	62
colspan friend(s)
Going to School	Storybox/Wright Group	A	46
Playground Fun	Troll	B	177
colspan frightened
I Am Frightened	Storybox/Wright Group	A	44
colspan from*
Happy Birthday	Literacy 2000/Rigby	A	35
colspan full
Danger	Storybox/Wright Group	A	68
colspan fun
Playground Fun	Troll	B	177
colspan get
Sunrise	Literacy 2000/Rigby	A	47
Here Comes Winter	Troll	B	241
Lilly-Lolly Little Legs	Literacy 2000/Rigby	B	133

Title (Author)	Series/Publisher	Level	Number of Words
give			
On the Farm	Literacy 2000/Rigby	A	21
Teeny Tiny (Bennett)	Houghton Mifflin	C	388
The Teeny Tiny Woman (Galdone)	Clarion Books	C	436
go			
Down to Town	Sunshine/Wright Group	A	29
Copy-Cat	Storybox/Wright Group	A	71
Little Pig	Storybox/Wright Group	A	56
Monster Meals	Literacy 2000/Rigby	A	35
Yuk Soup	Sunshine/Wright Group	A	27
Sleeping Out	Storybox/Wright Group	A	54
To Town	Storybox/Wright Group	B	147
Umbrella Parade	Troll	B	158
goes			
Wheels on the Bus (Raffi)	Crown	A	228
going			
The Race	Sunshine/Wright Group	A	27
Sleeping Out	Storybox/Wright Group	A	54
Where Are You Going, Aja Rose?	Sunshine/Wright Group	A	106
good			
Good for You	Sunshine/Wright Group	A	47
Five Little Kittens	Troll	A	138
Home for a Puppy	Troll	B	187
goodnight			
Goodnight Moon (Brown)	Harper & Row	B	138
got			
The Bicycle	Storybox/Wright Group	A	31

Title (Author)	Series/Publisher	Level	Number of Words
got *(cont.)*			
Happy Birthday	Literacy 2000/Rigby	A	35
Baby's Birthday	Literacy 2000/Rigby	A	53
Goodbye, Lucy	Sunshine/Wright Group	A	62
grew			
Bubble Gum in the Sky	Troll	B	139
Papa, Please Get the Moon for Me (Carle)	Picture Book Studio	C	242
grow			
The Seed	Sunshine/Wright Group	A	53
guess			
I Know an Old Lady (Bonne)	Rand McNally	B	422
happened			
The Very Quiet Cricket (Carle)	Philomel Books	C	324
has			
What Has Spots?	Literacy 2000/Rigby	A	36
Animals at the Zoo	Troll	B	158
have*			
Big and Little	Sunshine/Wright Group	A	35
Let's Have a Swim	Sunshine/Wright Group	A	78
Bread	Sunshine/Wright Group	A	70
The Pumpkin	Storybox/Wright Group	A	58
What Do You Have?	Tiger Cub/Peguis	B	179
Here Comes Winter	Troll	B	241
he*			
Little Brother	Sunshine/Wright Group	A	16
Plop!	Storybox/Wright Group	A	32
Happy Birthday	Literacy 2000/Rigby	A	35

Title (Author)	Series/Publisher	Level	Number of Words
he* *(cont.)*			
Too Big for Me	Storybox/Wright Group	A	77
Sticky Stanley	Troll	B	97
Obadiah	Storybox/Wright Group	B	106
hear			
What Do You Hear?	Tiger Cub/Peguis	A	84
Polar Bear, Polar Bear, What Do You Hear? (Martin, Jr.)	Henry Holt	A	208
heard			
Three Dogs at My Door	DLM	B	244
help			
Sticky Stanley	Troll	B	97
The Big Enormous Turnip	LINK	C	452
helps			
Along Comes Jake	Sunshine/Wright Group	A	89
her			
Our Baby	Literacy 2000/Rigby	A	16
Getting Ready for the Ball	Literacy 2000/Rigby	A	32
The Very Busy Spider (Carle)	Philomel Books	B	273
here			
My Home	Storybox/Wright Group	A	48
Five Little Kittens	Troll	A	138
Here Are My Hands (Martin, Jr.)	Henry Holt	B	100
Umbrella Parade	Troll	B	158
Elephant in Trouble	Troll	B	101
A Bath for a Beagle	Troll	B	107
Come and Have Fun (Hurd)	Harper & Row	C	436

Title (Author)	Series/Publisher	Level	Number of Words
he's			
Look for Me	Storybox/Wright Group	A	74
A Bath for a Beagle	Troll	B	107
Baby Panda at the Fair	DLM	C	164
hid/hide			
Easter Bunny's Lost Egg	Troll	B	178
high			
Come On Up!	Troll	B	136
him			
Look for Me	Storybox/Wright Group	A	74
Watch Your Step, Mr. Rabbit (Scarry)	Random House	B	98
his*			
If You Meet a Dragon	Storybox/Wright Group	A	31
home			
My Home	Sunshine/Wright Group	A	48
My Home	Storybox/Wright Group	A	48
Little Pig	Storybox/Wright Group	A	56
The Red Rose	Storybox/Wright Group	A	129
Home for a Puppy	Troll	B	197
house			
Our Street	Sunshine/Wright Group	A	42
I*			
Go, Go, Go	Storybox/Wright Group	A	22
I Love My Family	Sunshine/Wright Group	A	35
At the Zoo	DLM	A	153
What Can You See?	Tiger Cub/Peguis	A	73
I Can Spell Dinosaur	DLM	A	152
I Love Ladybugs	DLM	A	143

Title (Author)	Series/Publisher	Level	Number of Words
I'd			
If I Were a Fish	DLM	B	218
if			
Dan, the Flying Man	Storybox/Wright Group	A	64
If I Were a Fish	DLM	B	218
I'll			
What a Mess!	Storybox/Wright Group	A	56
Grumpy Elephant	Storybox/Wright Group	A	103
Oh, Jump in a Sack	Storybox/Wright Group	A	130
Fizz and Splutter	Storybox/Wright Group	A	113
Don't You Laugh at Me	Sunshine/Wright Group	A	175
The Penguins Come to Dinner	DLM	C	576
I'm			
I'm Bigger Than You	Sunshine/Wright Group	A	52
Three Dogs at My Door	DLM	B	244
Lilly-Lolly Little Legs	Literacy 2000/Rigby	B	133
in*			
The Bee	Storybox/Wright Group	A	28
Flying	Storybox/Wright Group	A	27
Jack-in-the-Box	Literacy 2000/Rigby	A	38
Yuk Soup	Sunshine/Wright Group	A	27
Night-Time	Storybox/Wright Group	A	48
Houses	Storybox/Wright Group	A	61
Teeny Tiny Tina	Literacy 2000/Rigby	A	34
I Spy	Literacy 2000/Rigby	A	27
Monster Meals	Literacy 2000/Rigby	A	35
The Pet Parade	Literacy 2000/Rigby	A	33

Title (Author)	Series/Publisher	Level	Number of Words
in* (cont.)			
Mrs. Wishy Washy	Storybox/Wright Group	B	105
To Town	Storybox/Wright Group	B	147
Obadiah	Storybox/Wright Group	B	106
into			
Copy-Cat	Storybox/Wright Group	A	71
In My Room	Literacy 2000/Rigby	A	49
Here Comes Winter	Troll	B	241
is*			
Jack-in-the-Box	Literacy 2000/Rigby	A	38
What Is a Huggles?	Sunshine/Wright Group	A	45
Our Street	Sunshine/Wright Group	A	42
What Is This?	Tiger Cub/Peguis	A	63
Houses	Storybox/Wright Group	A	61
Where Are They Going?	Storybox/Wright Group	A	46
My Home	Storybox/Wright Group	A	48
Night-Time	Storybox/Wright Group	A	48
The Jigaree	Storybox/Wright Group	B	130
Little Danny Dinosaur	Troll	B	198
Here Are My Hands (Martin, Jr.)	Henry Holt	B	100
it*			
Mud Pie	Literacy 2000/Rigby	A	16
A Monster Sandwich	Storybox/Wright Group	A	39
The Scarecrow	Literacy 2000/Rigby	A	33
The Jigaree	Storybox/Wright Group	B	130
Mrs. Wishy Washy	Storybox/Wright Group	B	105
Peanut Butter and Jelly (Westcott)	E. P. Dutton	B	156

Title (Author)	Series/Publisher	Level	Number of Words
I've			
Where Are You Going, Aja Rose?	Sunshine/Wright Group	A	106
Flying High	DLM	C	318
The Maligned Mosquito	DLM	C	447
jumped			
Let's Have a Swim	Sunshine/Wright Group	A	78
Obadiah	Storybox/Wright Group	B	106
jumping			
Five Little Monkeys Jumping on the Bed (Christelow)	Clarion Books	B	207
just			
Just Like Daddy (Asch)	Scholastic	B	96
Just for You (Mayer)	Golden Book	B	163
know			
I Know an Old Lady (Bonne)	Rand McNally	B	422
There's a Dragon in My Wagon (Nelson)	Modern Curriculum Press	B	77
Mongon	DLM	C	279
There Was an Old Lady	Child's Play (International)	C	189
last			
In My Room	Literacy 2000/Rigby	A	49
like			
My Home	Sunshine/Wright Group	A	48
I Like	Literacy 2000/Rigby	A	26
Ice Cream	Sunshine/Wright Group	A	51
At the Zoo	DLM	A	153
What Would You Like?	Sunshine/Wright Group	A	54

Title (Author)	Series/Publisher	Level	Number of Words
like *(cont.)*			
It Looked Like Spilt Milk (Shaw)	Harper & Row	B	177
I Love You, Good Night (Buller)	Simon & Schuster	B	101
Animals at the Zoo	Troll	B	158
Mud Pies	Troll	B	157
The Mixed-Up Chameleon (Carle)	Harper & Row	C	280
liked			
The Big Brown Teddy Bear	DLM	C	283
likes			
Our Dog Sam	Literacy 2000/Rigby	A	60
Skating on Thin Ice	Troll	B	134
little			
Big and Little	Sunshine/Wright Group	A	35
On a Chair	Storybox/Wright Group	A	33
Blue Sea (Kalan)	Greenwillow Books	A	74
Animals at the Zoo	Troll	B	158
Little Danny Dinosaur	Troll	B	198
The Big Brown Teddy Bear	DLM	C	283
At the Carnival	DLM	C	376
The Very Quiet Cricket (Carle)	Philomel Books	C	324
Three Billy Goats Gruff	Scholastic	C	399
live			
Where Do You Live?	Tiger Cub/Peguis	A	145
The Haunted House	Storybox/Wright Group	A	80
lived			
Over in the Meadow (Keats)	Scholastic	C	394

Title (Author)	Series/Publisher	Level	Number of Words
look			
On a Chair	Storybox/Wright Group	A	33
Where Are They Going?	Storybox/Wright Group	A	46
Danger	Storybox/Wright Group	A	68
Dizzy Lizzy	Literacy 2000/Rigby	B	37
Beautiful Breezy Blue and White Day	DLM	C	195
looked			
Look for Me	Storybox/Wright Group	A	74
It Looked Like Spilt Milk (Shaw)	Harper & Row	B	177
looking			
Brown Bear, Brown Bear, What Do You See? (Martin, Jr.)	Holt, Rinehart & Winston	A	201
Green Eyes	Literacy 2000/Rigby	B	113
Watch Your Step, Mr. Rabbit (Scarry)	Random House	B	98
love(s)			
I Love My Family	Sunshine/Wright Group	A	35
I Love Ladybugs	DLM	A	143
Ants Love Picnics Too	Literacy 2000/Rigby	A	31
made			
Little Brother	Storybox/Wright Group	A	33
Puppet Show	Troll	B	105
Sam the Scarecrow	Troll	B	146
makes			
The Wind Blows Strong	Sunshine/Wright Group	A	119
Fizz and Splutter	Storybox/Wright Group	A	113
Friendly Snowman	Troll	B	146
Birthday Buddies	Troll	B	173

Title (Author)	Series/Publisher	Level	Number of Words
makes *(cont.)*			
Mud Pies	Troll	B	157
The Doorbell Rang (Hutchins)	Scholastic	C	283
making			
Noisy Neighbors	Troll	C	428
maybe			
Baby Panda at the Fair	DLM	C	164
me			
Come with Me	Storybox/Wright Group	A	28
Dan, the Flying Man	Storybox/Wright Group	A	64
Sharing	Literacy 2000/Rigby	A	25
Too Big for Me	Storybox/Wright Group	A	77
Spider, Spider	Sunshine/Wright Group	A	72
No, No	Storybox/Wright Group	A	93
moon			
Goodnight Moon (Brown)	Harper & Row	B	138
Harold and the Purple Crayon (Harper)	Scholastic	C	662
more			
More and More Clowns	DLM	B	253
mother			
Who Will Be My Mother?	Storybox/Wright Group	B	160
Mother, Mother, I Want Another (Poluskin)	Crown	C	232
Are You My Mother? (Eastman)	Random House	C	703
much			
Noisy Neighbors	Troll	C	428
How Much Is a Million? (Schwartz)	Scholastic	C	300

Title (Author)	Series/Publisher	Level	Number of Words
my			
My Puppy	Sunshine/Wright Group	A	16
My Home	Sunshine/Wright Group	A	48
I Love My Family	Sunshine/Wright Group	A	35
Lost	Storybox/Wright Group	A	39
My Home	Storybox/Wright Group	A	48
All of Me	Literacy 2000/Rigby	A	28
In the Mirror	Storybox/Wright Group	A	26
Going to School	Storybox/Wright Group	A	46
In My Bed	Literacy 2000/Rigby	A	60
In My Room	Literacy 2000/Rigby	A	49
I Love Ladybugs	DLM	A	143
Snowflakes	Kaeden	A	56
Here Are My Hands (Martin, Jr.)	Henry Holt	B	100
There's a Dragon in My Wagon (Nelson)	Modern Curriculum Press	B	77
Red Is Best (Stinson)	Firefly Books	C	312
need			
Friendly Snowman	Troll	B	146
Lilly-Lolly Little Legs	Literacy 2000/Rigby	B	133
never			
Should You Ever?	Tiger Cub/Peguis	A	75
Flying High	DLM	C	318
night			
In My Room	Literacy 2000/Rigby	A	49
no			
My Puppy	Sunshine/Wright Group	A	16
Little Pig	Storybox/Wright Group	A	56

Title (Author)	Series/Publisher	Level	Number of Words
no *(cont.)*			
What Goes in the Bathtub?	Literacy 2000/Rigby	A	36
The Race	Sunshine/Wright Group	A	27
No, No	Storybox/Wright Group	A	93
I'm Bigger Than You	Sunshine/Wright Group	A	52
Horace	Storybox/Wright Group	A	57
Look for Me	Storybox/Wright Group	A	74
What Do You Do?	Tiger Cub/Peguis	A	162
What Do You Have?	Tiger Cub/Peguis	B	179
Little Danny Dinosaur	Troll	B	198
The Surprise	Literacy 2000/Rigby	B	126
No, No Joan (Bright)	School Book Fairs	B	110
noise			
Noisy Neighbors	Troll	C	428
not			
What Is a Huggles?	Sunshine/Wright Group	A	45
What's for Lunch?	Storybox/Wright Group	A	39
What Goes in the Bathtub?	Literacy 2000/Rigby	A	36
Look for Me	Storybox/Wright Group	A	74
Spider, Spider	Sunshine/Wright Group	A	72
Fizz and Splutter	Storybox/Wright Group	A	113
A Bath for a Beagle	Troll	B	107
Little Danny Dinosaur	Troll	B	198
Green Eyes	Literacy 2000/Rigby	B	113
nothing			
The Carrot Seed (Krauss)	Scholastic	B	104

Title (Author)	Series/Publisher	Level	Number of Words
nothing *(cont.)*			
Don't You Laugh at Me	Sunshine/Wright Group	A	175
o'clock			
The Grouchy Ladybug (Carle)	Harper & Row	C	822
of*			
The Bee	Storybox/Wright Group	A	28
I Am Frightened	Storybox/Wright Group	A	44
The Birthday Cake	Literacy 2000/Rigby	A	27
Danger	Storybox/Wright Group	A	68
Have You Seen?	Literacy 2000/Rigby	B	41
More and More Clowns	DLM	B	253
off			
Five Little Monkeys Jumping on the Bed (Christelow)	Clarion Books	B	207
oh			
Horace	Storybox/Wright Group	A	57
Mrs. Wishy Washy	Storybox/Wright Group	B	105
Oh, Jump in a Sack	Storybox/Wright Group	B	130
old			
Fizz and Splutter	Storybox/Wright Group	A	113
I Know an Old Lady (Bonne)	Rand McNally	B	422
There Was an Old Lady	Child's Play(International)	C	189
on*			
Dressing Up	Literacy 2000/Rigby	A	43
The Bicycle	Storybox/Wright Group	A	31
A Monster Sandwich	Storybox/Wright Group	A	39
The Long, Long Tail	Sunshine/Wright Group	A	37
Stop!	Storybox/Wright Group	A	55

Title (Author)	Series/Publisher	Level	Number of Words
on* *(cont.)*			
Snowflakes	Kaeden	A	56
The Clown	Kaeden	A	31
Wheels	Literacy 2000/Rigby	A	27
once			
Chicken Soup with Rice (Sendak)	Scholastic	C	366
one			
Sharing	Literacy 2000/Rigby	A	25
One Light, One Sun (Raffi)	Crown	B	65
Three Dogs at My Door	DLM	B	244
A Rhinoceros? Preposterous!	DLM	C	438
only			
Freddie the Frog	Troll	B	145
or			
Don't You Laugh at Me	Sunshine/Wright Group	A	175
Marvelous Me	Literacy 2000/Rigby	B	34
Oh, Jump in a Sack	Storybox/Wright Group	B	130
our			
Our Dog Sam	Literacy 2000/Rigby	A	60
out			
The Bee	Storybox/Wright Group	A	28
Flying	Storybox/Wright Group	A	27
Let's Have a Swim	Sunshine/Wright Group	A	78
Danger	Storybox/Wright Group	A	68
More and More Clowns	DLM	B	253
Watch Your Step, Mr. Rabbit (Scarry)	Random House	B	98
over			
On a Chair	Storybox/Wright Group	A	33

Title (Author)	Series/Publisher	Level	Number of Words
over *(cont.)*			
Dan, the Flying Man	Storybox/Wright Group	A	64
The Monkey Bridge	Sunshine/Wright Group	A	66
Over in the Meadow (Keats)	Scholastic	C	394
perhaps			
Baby Panda at the Fair	DLM	C	164
There Was an Old Lady	Child's Play (International)	C	189
play(ed)			
Five Little Kittens	Troll	A	138
What Can You Do?	Tiger Cub/Peguis	A	61
The Marching Band	Kaeden	A	38
Baby's Birthday	Literacy 2000/Rigby	A	53
please			
Pancakes for Supper	Literacy 2000/Rigby	B	99
pull(ed)			
The Big Enormous Turnip	LINK	C	452
puppy			
My Puppy	Sunshine/Wright Group	A	16
Home for a Puppy	Troll	B	197
put(s)			
Dressing Up	Literacy 2000/Rigby	A	43
A Monster Sandwich	Storybox/Wright Group	A	39
Shark in a Sack	Sunshine/Wright Group	A	69
The Clown	Kaeden	A	31
Rub-a-Dub Suds	Troll	B	152
I Was Walking Down the Road (Barchas)	Scholastic	B	305

Title (Author)	Series/Publisher	Level	Number of Words
ran			
Two Little Dogs	Storybox/Wright Group	A	74
really			
The Maligned Mosquito	DLM	C	447
right			
Horace	Storybox/Wright Group	A	57
Birthday Buddies	Troll	B	173
room			
In My Bed	Literacy 2000/Rigby	A	60
In My Room	Literacy 2000/Rigby	A	49
round			
Round and Round	Storybox/Wright Group	A	38
Wheels on the Bus (Raffi)	Crown	A	228
run			
What a Dog!	Troll	B	137
said			
The Chocolate Cake	Storybox/Wright Group	A	26
My Home	Sunshine/Wright Group	A	48
My Home	Storybox/Wright Group	A	48
Sunrise	Literacy 2000/Rigby	A	47
What's for Lunch?	Storybox/Wright Group	A	39
Little Pig	Storybox/Wright Group	A	56
The Red Rose	Storybox/Wright Group	A	129
"Scat!" Said the Cat	Sunshine/Wright Group	A	37
Too Big for Me	Storybox/Wright Group	A	77
Look for Me	Storybox/Wright Group	A	74
Horace	Storybox/Wright Group	A	57
What A Mess!	Storybox/Wright Group	A	56

Title (Author)	Series/Publisher	Level	Number of Words
said *(cont.)*			
At the Zoo	DLM	A	153
Mrs. Wishy Washy	Storybox/Wright Group	B	105
Freddie the Frog	Troll	B	145
Five Little Monkeys Jumping on the Bed (Christelow)	Clarion Books	B	207
Over in the Meadow (Keats)	Scholastic	C	394
Miss Nelson Is Missing (Allard)	Houghton Mifflin	C	596
Three Billy Goats Gruff	Scholastic	C	399
The Grouchy Ladybug (Carle)	Harper & Row	C	822
saw			
Bread	Sunshine/Wright Group	A	70
I Was Walking Down the Road (Barchas)	Scholastic	B	305
I Saw a Dinosaur	Literacy 2000/Rigby	B	59
say			
The Monster Under My Bed	Troll	B	203
Down By the Bay (Raffi)	Crown	B	248
says			
Hello	Storybox/Wright Group	A	66
Five Little Kittens	Troll	A	138
What a Dog!	Troll	B	137
Muffy and Fluffy	Troll	B	159
Red Is Best (Stinson)	Firefly Books	C	312
Mongon	DLM	C	279
scared			
The Scarecrow	Literacy 2000/Rigby	A	33
Sam the Scarecrow	Troll	B	146

Title (Author)	Series/Publisher	Level	Number of Words
see			
In the Mirror	Storybox/Wright Group	A	26
All of Me	Literacy 2000/Rigby	A	28
Up in a Tree	Sunshine/Wright Group	A	51
The Ghost	Storybox/Wright Group	A	26
Plop!	Storybox/Wright Group	A	32
What Can You See?	Tiger Cub/Peguis	A	73
The Red Rose	Storybox/Wright Group	A	129
Brown Bear, Brown Bear, What Do You See? (Martin, Jr.)	Holt, Rinehart & Winston	A	201
The Jigaree	Storybox/Wright Group	B	130
See You Later, Alligator (Strauss)	Price Stern Sloan	B	131
sees			
Up in a Tree	Sunshine/Wright Group	A	51
she			
Our Granny	Sunshine/Wright Group	A	43
Look for Me	Storybox/Wright Group	A	74
When Itchy Witchy Sneezes	Sunshine/Wright Group	A	43
Where Is Nancy?	Literacy 2000/Rigby	B	59
Sticky Stanley	Troll	B	97
I Know an Old Lady (Bonne)	Rand McNally	B	422
The Very Busy Spider (Carle)	Philomel Books	B	273
she'll			
There Was an Old Lady	Child's Play (International)	C	189
should			
Should You Ever?	Tiger Cub/Peguis	A	75
sleep			
Sleeping Out	Storybox/Wright Group	A	54

Title (Author)	Series/Publisher	Level	Number of Words
smaller			
Papa, Please Get the Moon for Me (Carle)	Picture Book Studio	C	242
so			
Horace	Storybox/Wright Group	A	57
Teeny Tiny (Bennett)	Houghton Mifflin	C	388
The Teeny Tiny Woman (Galdone)	Clarion	C	436
some			
Huggles Goes Away	Sunshine/Wright Group	A	17
A Monster Sandwich	Storybox/Wright Group	A	39
Fruit Salad	Literacy 2000/Rigby	A	17
A Scrumptious Sundae	Literacy 2000/Rigby	A	21
Yuk Soup	Sunshine/Wright Group	A	27
Bread	Sunshine/Wright Group	A	70
Mud Pies	Troll	B	157
Let's Get a Pet	Troll	B	148
something			
Goodbye, Lucy	Sunshine/Wright Group	A	62
sometimes			
It Looked Like Spilt Milk (Shaw)	Harper & Row	B	177
Skating on Thin Ice	Troll	B	134
talk			
No, No	Storybox/Wright Group	A	93
tells			
Snap!	Sunshine/Wright Group	A	32
than			
I'm Bigger Than You	Sunshine/Wright Group	A	52

Title (Author)	Series/Publisher	Level	Number of Words
that*			
Sleeping Out	Storybox/Wright Group	A	54
Come On Up!	Troll	B	136
The Monster Under My Bed	Troll	B	203
Three Billy Goats Gruff	Scholastic	C	399
The Penguins Come to Dinner	DLM	C	576
that's			
Fizz and Splutter	Storybox/Wright Group	A	113
A Dream in a Wishing Well	DLM	B	399
The Doorbell Rang (Hutchins)	Scholastic	C	283
the*			
Painting	Storybox/Wright Group	A	25
Baby Gets Dressed	Sunshine/Wright Group	A	19
The Circus	Literacy 2000/Rigby	A	16
The Farm	Literacy 2000/Rigby	A	16
The Ghost	Storybox/Wright Group	A	26
their			
Wake Up, Mom	Sunshine/Wright Group	A	94
them			
Peanut Butter and Jelly (Westcott)	E. P. Dutton	B	156
then			
Getting Ready for the Ball	Literacy 2000/Rigby	A	32
Along Comes Jake	Sunshine/Wright Group	A	89
Too Many Clothes	Literacy 2000/Rigby	A	27
Peanut Butter and Jelly (Westcott)	E. P. Dutton	B	156
I Was Walking Down the Road (Barchas)	Scholastic	B	305
Bear's Busy Year	Troll	C	300

Title (Author)	Series/Publisher	Level	Number of Words
there			
On a Chair	Storybox/Wright Group	A	33
Houses	Storybox/Wright Group	A	61
Uncle Buncle's House	Sunshine/Wright Group	A	59
The Jigaree	Storybox/Wright Group	B	130
Cookie's Week (Ward)	Scholastic	B	85
Playground Fun	Troll	B	177
At the Carnival	DLM	C	376
There Was an Old Lady	Child's Play (International)	C	189
there's			
In My Bed	Literacy 2000/Rigby	A	60
There's a Dragon in My Wagon (Nelson)	Modern Curriculum Press	B	77
Beautiful Breezy Blue and White Day	DLM	C	195
they*			
Dressing Up	Literacy 2000/Rigby	A	43
Buzzing Flies	Sunshine/Wright Group	A	47
The Night-Train	Storybox/Wright Group	A	74
The Seed	Sunshine/Wright Group	A	53
Danger	Storybox/Wright Group	A	68
Two Little Dogs	Storybox/Wright Group	A	74
Bread	Sunshine/Wright Group	A	70
Muffy and Fluffy	Troll	B	159
Let's Get a Pet	Troll	B	148
What a Dog!	Troll	B	137
Mongon	DLM	C	279
The Penguins Come to Dinner	DLM	C	576

Title (Author)	Series/Publisher	Level	Number of Words
thing			
Where Are They Going?	Storybox/Wright Group	A	46
Noises	Literacy 2000/Rigby	B	50
things			
Where the Wild Things Are (Sendak)	Harper & Row	C	344
this*			
Our Street	Sunshine/Wright Group	A	42
What Is This?	Tiger Cub/Peguis	A	63
The Cement Tent	Troll	B	96
What Has Spots?	Literacy 2000/Rigby	B	36
Noisy Neighbors	Troll	C	428
time			
Sunrise	Literacy 2000/Rigby	A	47
to*			
Going to School	Storybox/Wright Group	A	46
Too Big for Me	Storybox/Wright Group	A	77
Sleeping Out	Storybox/Wright Group	A	54
Sunrise	Literacy 2000/Rigby	A	47
Hello	Storybox/Wright Group	A	66
Our Dog Sam	Literacy 2000/Rigby	A	60
No, No, Joan (Bright)	School Book Fairs	B	11
Who Will Be My Mother?	Storybox/Wright Group	B	160
To Town	Storybox/Wright Group	B	147
together			
The Very Quiet Cricket (Carle)	Philomel Books	C	324
too			
Ants Love Picnics Too	Literacy 2000/Rigby	A	31
Come On Up!	Troll	B	136

Title (Author)	Series/Publisher	Level	Number of Words
too *(cont.)*			
Just for You (Mayer)	Golden Book	B	163
town			
Wheels on the Bus (Raffi)	Crown	B	228
tried			
Sticky Stanley	Troll	B	97
Freddie the Frog	Troll	B	145
turns			
The Monster Under My Bed	Troll	B	203
twice			
Chicken Soup with Rice (Sendak)	Scholastic	C	366
up			
The Tree House	Storybox/Wright Group	A	35
Dinner!	Sunshine/Wright Group	A	20
I Can Fly	Sunshine/Wright Group	A	24
Copy-Cat	Storybox/Wright Group	A	71
Flying	Storybox/Wright Group	A	27
Sunrise	Literacy 2000/Rigby	A	47
I Am a Bookworm	Sunshine/Wright Group	A	36
Up in a Tree	Sunshine/Wright Group	A	51
Come On Up!	Troll	B	136
The Carrot Seed (Krauss)	Scholastic	B	104
Pancakes for Supper	Literacy 2000/Rigby	B	99
very			
Little Danny Dinosaur	Troll	B	198
The Very Busy Spider (Carle)	Philomel Books	B	273
Let's Get a Pet	Troll	B	148
The Maligned Mosquito	DLM	C	447

Title (Author)	Series/Publisher	Level	Number of Words
very *(cont.)*			
Papa, Please Get the Moon for Me (Carle)	Picture Book Studio	C	242
want(s)			
Lost	Storybox/Wright Group	A	39
Wake Up, Mom	Sunshine/Wright Group	A	94
Fizz and Splutter	Storybox/Wright Group	A	113
No, No, Joan (Bright)	School Book Fairs	A	110
Little Danny Dinosaur	Troll	B	198
The Very Busy Spider (Carle)	Philomel Books	B	273
Mother, Mother, I Want Another (Poluskin)	Crown	C	232
The Grouchy Ladybug (Carle)	Harper & Row	C	822
wanted			
Just for You (Mayer)	Golden Book	B	163
The Very Quiet Cricket (Carle)	Philomel Books	C	324
warm			
A Hug Is Warm	Sunshine/Wright Group	A	64
was*			
When I Was Sick	Literacy 2000/Rigby	A	74
Cookie's Week (Ward)	Scholastic	B	85
The Very Busy Spider (Carle)	Philomel Books	B	273
Three Dogs at My Door	DLM	B	244
Obadiah	Storybox/Wright Group	B	196
Sam the Scarecrow	Troll	B	146
The Big Brown Teddy Bear	DLM	C	283
There Was an Old Lady	Child's Play (International)	C	189
wasn't			
Timmy	Literacy 2000/Rigby	B	56

Title (Author)	Series/Publisher	Level	Number of Words
watch			
Watch Out!	Literacy 2000/Rigby	A	29
wave			
Going to School	Storybox/Wright Group	A	46
way			
To Town	Storybox/Wright Group	B	147
we			
Ice Cream	Sunshine/Wright Group	A	51
The Big Hill	Storybox/Wright Group	A	22
Puppet Show	Troll	B	105
Friendly Snowman	Troll	B	146
Watch Your Step, Mr. Rabbit (Scarry)	Random House	B	98
Scruffy Messed It Up	Literacy 2000/Rigby	B	109
we'll			
The Pumpkin	Storybox/Wright Group	A	58
went			
The Tree House	Storybox/Wright Group	A	35
Shoo!	Sunshine/Wright Group	A	38
Stop!	Storybox/Wright Group	A	55
The Red Rose	Storybox/Wright Group	A	129
Oh, Jump in a Sack	Storybox/Wright Group	A	130
The Farm Concert	Storybox/Wright Group	A	77
The Monkey Bridge	Sunshine/Wright Group	A	66
Mrs. Wishy Washy	Storybox/Wright Group	B	105
Who Will Be My Mother?	Storybox/Wright Group	B	160
The Dinosaur Ball	DLM	C	294
were			
If I Were a Fish	DLM	B	218

Title (Author)	Series/Publisher	Level	Number of Words
we're			
The Race	Sunshine/Wright Group	A	27
wet			
Elephant in Trouble	Troll	B	101
what			
Up in a Tree	Sunshine/Wright Group	A	51
The Monsters' Party	Storybox/Wright Group	A	95
What a Mess!	Storybox/Wright Group	A	56
Too Big for Me	Storybox/Wright Group	A	77
Fizz and Splutter	Storybox/Wright Group	A	113
Brown Bear, Brown Bear, What Do You See? (Martin, Jr.)	Holt, Rinehart & Winston	A	201
Polar Bear, Polar Bear, What Do You Hear? (Martin, Jr.)	Henry Holt	A	208
The Monster Under My Bed	Troll	B	203
Here Comes Winter	Troll	B	241
The Big Brown Teddy Bear	DLM	C	283
what's			
What's for Lunch?	Storybox/Wright Group	A	39
Sleeping Out	Storybox/Wright Group	A	54
when			
When I Play	Literacy 2000/Rigby	A	34
When I Was Sick	Literacy 2000/Rigby	A	74
Our Granny	Sunshine/Wright Group	A	43
Three Dogs at My Door	DLM	B	244
Teeny Tiny (Bennett)	Houghton Mifflin	C	388
The Teeny Tiny Woman (Galdone)	Clarion Books	C	436

Title (Author)	Series/Publisher	Level	Number of Words
whenever			
The Maligned Mosquito	DLM	C	447
where			
On a Chair	Storybox/Wright Group	A	33
Where Are They Going?	Storybox/Wright Group	A	46
Where Are You Going, Aja Rose?	Sunshine/Wright Group	A	106
Where Do You Live?	Tiger Cub/Peguis	A	145
Down By the Bay (Raffi)	Crown	B	248
Easter Bunny's Lost Egg	Troll	B	178
Whose Mouse Are You? (Kraus)	Scholastic	B	109
Come and Have Fun (Hurd)	Harper & Row	C	436
Where the Wild Things Are (Sendak)	Harper & Row	C	344
who			
Who Lives Here?	Storybox/Wright Group	A	31
Mr. Grump	Storybox/Wright Group	A	75
Who Cried for Pie?	Troll	A	90
I Know an Old Lady (Bonne)	Rand McNally	B	422
who's			
Three Billy Goats Gruff	Scholastic	C	399
why			
Come for a Swim	Sunshine/Wright Group	A	134
Q Is for Duck (Etling)	Clarion Books	B	242
I Know an Old Lady (Bonne)	Rand McNally	B	422
The Maligned Mosquito	DLM	C	447
The Penguins Come to Dinner	DLM	C	576
Noisy Neighbors	Troll	C	428
There Was an Old Lady	Child's Play (International)	C	189

Title (Author)	Series/Publisher	Level	Number of Words
will			
Should You Ever?	Tiger Cub/Peguis	A	75
Friendly Snowman	Troll	B	146
The Surprise	Literacy 2000/Rigby	B	126
Let's Get a Pet	Troll	B	148
To Town	Storybox/Wright Group	B	147
win			
The Race	Sunshine/Wright Group	A	27
wish			
The Mixed-Up Chameleon (Carle)	Harper & Row	C	280
with*			
Come with Me	Storybox/Wright Group	A	28
Along Comes Jake	Sunshine/Wright Group	A	89
The Old Steam Train	Literacy 2000/Rigby	B	46
Umbrella Parade	Troll	B	158
A Dream in a Wishing Well	DLM	B	399
At the Carnival	DLM	C	376
Chicken Soup with Rice (Sendak)	Scholastic	C	366
won't			
Oh, Jump in a Sack	Storybox/Wright Group	A	130
The Carrot Seed (Krauss)	Scholastic	B	104
would/wouldn't			
What Would You Like?	Sunshine/Wright Group	A	54
you			
Sharing	Literacy 2000/Rigby	A	25
Copy-Cat	Storybox/Wright Group	A	71
Dan, the Flying Man	Storybox/Wright Group	A	64
Horace	Storybox/Wright Group	A	57

Title (Author)	Series/Publisher	Level	Number of Words
you *(cont.)*			
Shark in a Sack	Sunshine/Wright Group	A	69
I'm Bigger Than You	Sunshine/Wright Group	A	52
Good for You	Sunshine/Wright Group	A	47
At the Zoo	DLM	A	153
Where Do You Live?	Tiger Cub/Peguis	A	145
What Do You Do?	Tiger Cub/Peguis	A	162
Brown Bear, Brown Bear, What Do You See? (Martin, Jr.)	Holt, Rinehart & Winston	A	201
Polar Bear, Polar Bear, What Do You Hear? (Martin, Jr.)	Henry Holt	A	208
What Do You Have?	Tiger Cub/Peguis	B	179
Lilly-Lolly Little Legs	Literacy 2000/Rigby	B	133
Animals at the Zoo	Troll	B	158
Let's Get a Pet	Troll	B	148
Just for You (Mayer)	Golden Book	B	163
Who Will Be My Mother?	Storybox/Wright Group	B	160
I Love You, Good Night (Buller)	Simon & Schuster	B	101
your			
What a Mess!	Storybox/Wright Group	A	56
The Clown	Kaeden	A	31
Goodbye, Lucy	Sunshine/Wright Group	A	62
Whose Mouse Are You? (Kraus)	Scholastic	B	109
Red Is Best (Stinson)	Firefly Books	C	312
you've			
Goodbye, Lucy	Sunshine/Wright Group	A	62

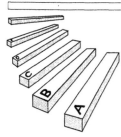

Chapter 4

Common Concepts

Title (Author)	Series/Publisher	Level	Number of Words
color words			
The Birthday Cake	Sunshine/Wright Group	A	25
Jack-in-the-Box	Literacy 2000/Rigby	A	38
Houses	Storybox/Wright Group	A	61
Brown Bear, Brown Bear, What Do You See? (Martin, Jr.)	Holt, Rinehart & Winston	A	201
Umbrella Parade	Troll	B	158
To Town	Storybox/Wright Group	B	147
Planting a Rainbow (Ehlert)	Harcourt Brace Jovanovich	B	127
The Very Hungry Caterpillar (Carle)	Philomel Books	C	228
Red Is Best (Stinson)	Firefly Books	C	312
Caps for Sale (Slobodkina)	Harper & Row	C	672
comparatives			
I'm Bigger Than You Are	Storybox/Wright Group	A	52
Blue Sea (Kalan)	Greenwillow Books	A	74
More and More Clowns	DLM	B	253
contractions			
I Love Ladybugs	DLM	A	143
Fizz and Splutter	Storybox/Wright Group	A	113
The Carrot Seed (Krauss)	Scholastic	B	104
Fix-It (McPhail)	E. P. Dutton	C	171

Title (Author)	Series/Publisher	Level	Number of Words
contractions (*cont.*)			
Leo the Late Bloomer (Kraus)	Windmill Books	C	168
There's a Nightmare in My Closet (Mayer)	Dial Books	C	159
If You Give a Mouse a Cookie (Numeroff)	Harper & Row	C	298
If You Give a Moose a Muffin (Numeroff)	Harper & Row	C	313
days of the week			
On Monday When It Rained (Kachenmeister)	Houghton Mifflin	B	242
Cookie's Week (Ward)	Scholastic	B	85
Mom's Haircut	Literacy 2000/Rigby	B	101
The Very Hungry Caterpillar (Carle)	Philomel Books	C	228
direction/position words			
Mouse	Storybox/Wright Group	A	61
Kittens	Literacy 2000/Rigby	A	23
Silly Old Possum	Storybox/Wright Group	A	44
Rosie's Walk (Hutchins)	Collier Books	B	34
The Secret Birthday Message (Carle)	Harper & Row	B	165
family names			
The Chocolate Cake	Storybox/Wright Group	A	26
Happy Birthday	Literacy 2000/Rigby	A	35
I Love My Family	Sunshine/Wright Group	A	35
Little Brother	Storybox/Wright Group	A	33
I Love Ladybugs	DLM	A	143
The Pumpkin	Storybox/Wright Group	A	58
Who Cried for Pie?	Troll	A	90
Mud Pies	Troll	B	157
Little Danny Dinosaur	Troll	B	198

Title (Author)	Series/Publisher	Level	Number of Words
family names (*cont.*)			
Whose Mouse Are You? (Kraus)	Scholastic	B	109
months of the year			
Chicken Soup with Rice (Sendak)	Scholastic	C	366
number words			
Who Lives Here?	Storybox/Wright Group	A	31
Ten Little Men	Literacy 2000/Rigby	A	38
One, One Is the Sun	Storybox/Wright Group	A	47
Uncle Buncle's House	Sunshine/Wright Group	A	59
The Monkey Bridge	Sunshine/Wright Group	A	66
Five Little Kittens	Troll	A	138
Five Little Monkeys Jumping on the Bed (Christelow)	Clarion Books	B	207
A Dream in a Wishing Well	DLM	B	399
Over in the Meadow (Keats)	Scholastic	C	394
The Very Hungry Caterpillar (Carle)	Philomel Books	C	228
The Dinosaur Ball	DLM	C	294
The Doorbell Rang (Hutchins)	Scholastic	C	283
opposites			
Snoopy's Book of Opposites (Hall)	Golden Book	A	59
The Kitten Twins	Troll	B	209
ordinal numbers			
Carla's New Friends	DLM	C	639
possessive			
Major Jump	Sunshine/Wright Group	A	24
Uncle Buncle's House	Sunshine/Wright Group	A	59
Whose Mouse Are You? (Kraus)	Scholastic	B	109

Title (Author)	Series/Publisher	Level	Number of Words
punctuation			
period			
I Want Ice Cream	Storybox/Wright Group	A	18
Go, Go, Go	Storybox/Wright Group	A	22
What Are You?	Literacy 2000/Rigby	A	30
Feet	Storybox/Wright Group	A	19
question mark			
Where Do You Live?	Tiger Cub/Peguis	A	145
"Scat!" Said the Cat	Sunshine/Wright Group	A	37
What Would You Like?	Sunshine/Wright Group	A	54
Up in a Tree	Sunshine/Wright Group	A	51
The Monsters' Party	Storybox/Wright Group	A	95
Brown Bear, Brown Bear, What Do You See? (Martin, Jr.)	Holt, Rinehart & Winston	A	201
Who Cried for Pie?	Troll	A	90
Polar Bear, Polar Bear, What Do You Hear? (Martin, Jr.)	Henry Holt	A	208
The Very Busy Spider (Carle)	Philomel Books	B	273
Animals at the Zoo	Troll	B	158
Little Danny Dinosaur	Troll	B	198
A Rhinoceros? Preposterous!	DLM	C	438
Sandcake (Asch)	Parents' Magazine Press	C	456
Are You My Mother? (Eastman)	Random House	C	703
The Grouchy Ladybug (Carle)	Harper & Row	C	822
exclamation point			
My Puppy	Sunshine/Wright Group	A	16
Where Are They Going?	Storybox/Wright Group	A	46
Splosh!	Storybox/Wright Group	A	48

Title (Author)	Series/Publisher	Level	Number of Words
exclamation point (*cont.*)			
The Chocolate Cake	Storybox/Wright Group	A	26
Goodbye, Lucy	Sunshine/Wright Group	A	62
A Rhinoceros? Preposterous!	DLM	C	438
comma			
Splosh!	Storybox/Wright Group	A	48
To New York	Storybox/Wright Group	A	37
A Scrumptious Sundae	Literacy 2000/Rigby	A	21
Huggles' Breakfast	Sunshine/Wright Group	A	16
Baby Gets Dressed	Sunshine/Wright Group	A	19
I Can Fly	Sunshine/Wright Group	A	24
Over in the Meadow (Keats)	Scholastic	B	394
Mother, Mother, I Want Another (Poluskin)	Crown	C	232
quotation marks			
Who's Going to Lick the Bowl?	Storybox/Wright Group	A	24
The Chocolate Cake	Storybox/Wright Group	A	26
Sunrise	Literacy 2000/Rigby	A	47
What A Mess!	Storybox/Wright Group	A	56
Little Pig	Storybox/Wright Group	A	56
The Farm Concert	Storybox/Wright Group	A	77
"Scat!" Said the Cat	Sunshine/Wright Group	A	37
Who Will Be My Mother?	Storybox/Wright Group	B	160
The Very Busy Spider (Carle)	Philomel Books	B	273
Freddie the Frog	Troll	B	145
Five Little Monkeys Jumping on the Bed (Christelow)	Clarion Books	B	207
Mongon	DLM	C	279

Title (Author)	Series/Publisher	Level	Number of Words
quotation marks (*cont.*)			
Mother, Mother, I Want Another (Poluskin)	Crown	C	232
Why Can't I Fly? (Gelman)	Scholastic	C	353
Miss Nelson Is Missing (Allard)	Houghton Mifflin	C	596
Three Billy Goats Gruff	Scholastic	C	399
ellipsis			
I Spy	Literacy 2000/Rigby	A	27
Cookie's Week (Ward)	Scholastic	B	85
Have You Seen?	Literacy 2000/Rigby	B	43

Personal Additions:

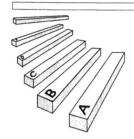

Appendix A

Phonics Generalizations

CVC: When a single vowel comes between two consonants, that vowel is usually short. [*cat*; *duck*; *still*]

CVVC: When two vowels appear together in a word, the first one is usually long and the second one is silent. [*boat*; *seem*; *eat*]

CVCe: When *e* is the final vowel in a word, the preceding vowel is usually long and the *e* is silent. [*cake*; *fine*; *tube*]

VC: When a single vowel is at the beginning of a word, it is usually short. [*am*; *on*; *ink*]

CV: When a single vowel is at the end of a word, it is often long. [*go*; *hi*; *be*]

Vowel Y: When **y** is at the end of a one-part word, it has the sound of long *i*; when **y** is at the end of a two-part word, it has the sound of long *e*. [*sky*; *funny*]

Blends: When two or more consonants appear together and each consonant can be heard in sequence, there is a consonant blend. [*blow*; *street*; *fist*]

Digraphs: When two consonants appear together and make one sound, there is a consonant digraph. [*much*; *shout*; *that*; *white*]

CK Digraph: When a short vowel word ends with the sound of *k*, use the *ck* digraph; when a long vowel word ends with the sound of *k*, use *k* alone. [*sick*; *bike*]

Diphthongs: When two vowels appear together and form an unsegmentable, varying, but single sound, there is a diphthong. [*boy*; *school*; *knew*]

R-controlled: When *r* follows a single vowel, it changes the sound that vowel would otherwise make. [car; fir; mother]

Soft and Hard g and c: When **g** or **c** is followed by an *i*, *e*, or *y*, it has a soft sound; when **g** or **c** is followed by an *a*, *o*, or *u*, or is the last letter of a word, it has a hard sound. [*giraffe*; *cement*; *cycle*; *bag*; *go*; *guess*]

ing ending: The suffix **ing** may be added to a base word to form nouns or to express a different verb tense. [*building*; *is jumping*]

ed ending: The suffix **ed** may be added to a base word to form adjectives or to express a past tense of a verb. [*bearded*; *walked*]

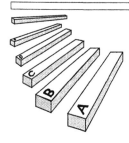

Appendix B

High-Frequency Words in Order of Frequency

The first 100 most commonly written words in order of frequency:

1. the	21. be	41. which	61. into	81. made
2. of	22. this	42. their	62. has	82. over
3. and	23. from	43. said	63. more	83. did
4. a	24. I	44. if	64. her	84. down
5. to	25. have	45. do	65. two	85. only
6. in	26. or	46. will	66. like	86. way
7. is	27. by	47. each	67. him	87. find
8. you	28. one	48. about	68. see	88. use
9. that	29. had	49. how	69. time	89. may
10. it	30. not	50. up	70. could	90. water
11. he	31. but	51. out	71. no	91. long
12. for	32. what	52. them	72. make	92. little
13. was	33. all	53. then	73. than	93. very
14. on	34. were	54. she	74. first	94. after
15. are	35. when	55. many	75. been	95. words
16. as	36. we	56. some	76. its	96. called
17. with	37. there	57. so	77. who	97. just
18. his	38. can	58. these	78. now	98. where
19. they	39. an	59. would	79. people	99. most
20. at	40. your	60. other	80. my	100. know

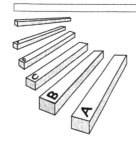

Appendix C

High-Frequency Words in Alphabetical Order

The first 100 most commonly written words in alphabetical order:

a, about, after, all, an, and, are, as, at

be, been, but, by

called, can, could

did, do, down

each

find, first, for, from

had, has, have, he, her, him, his, how

I, if, in, into, is, it, its

just

know

like, little, long

made, make, many, may, more, most, my

no, not, now

of, on, one, only, or, other, out, over

people

said, see, she, so, some

than, that, the, their, them, then, there, these, they, this, time, to, two

up, use

very

was, water, way, we, were, what, when, where, which, who, will, with, words, would

you, your

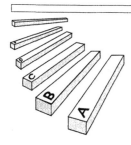

Appendix D

Basic Sight Vocabulary

List compiled by E. W. Dolch.

*a	cold	green	*my	*see	*two
*about	come	grow	myself	seven	under
*after	*could	*had	never	shall	*up
again	cut	*has	new	*she	upon
*all	*did	*have	*no	show	us
always	*do	*he	*not	sing	*use
am	does	help	*now	sit	*very
*an	done	*her	*of	six	walk
any	don't	here	off	sleep	want
*are	*down	*him	old	small	warm
around	draw	*his	*on	*so	*was
*as	drink	hold	once	*some	wash
ask	eat	hot	*one	soon	*we
*at	eight	*how	*only	start	well
ate	every	hurt	open	stop	went
away	fall	*I	*or	take	*were
*be	far	*if	our	tell	*what
because	fast	*in	*out	ten	*when
*been	*find	*into	*over	thank	*where
before	*first	*is	*own	*that	*which
best	five	*it	pick	*the	white
better	fly	*its	play	*their	*who
big	*for	laugh	please	*them	why
black	found	let	pretty	*then	*will
blue	four	light	pull	*there	wish
both	*from	*like	put	*these	*with
bring	full	*little	ran	*they	work
brown	funny	live	read	think	*would
*but	gave	*long	red	*this	write
buy	get	*made	ride	those	yellow
*by	give	*make	right	three	yes
call	go	*many	round	*to	*you
came	goes	*may	run	today	*your
*can	going	me	*said	together	
carry	good	much	saw	too	
clean	got	must	say	try	

*Word is also one of the first 100 most frequently written words.

The above list accounts for 70 percent of words found in books commonly leveled as first-grade readers, 66 percent of words found in books commonly leveled as second-grade readers, and 65 percent of words found in books commonly leveled as third-grade readers.

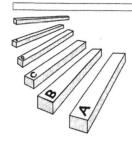

Appendix E

Publishers' Addresses

The following addresses may be helpful in contacting publishers about individual titles cited in this resource.

Clarion Books
215 Park Ave. South
New York, NY 10003

Crown Publishers
225 Park Ave. South
New York, NY 10003

DLM Teaching Resources
One DLM Park
Allen, TX 75002

Greenwillow Books
1350 Avenue of the Americas
New York, NY 10019

Harper & Row Publishers, Inc.
10 East 53rd Street
New York, NY 10022

Houghton Mifflin Co.
One Beacon Street
Boston, MA 02108

Henry Holt & Co.
115 West 18th Street
New York, NY 10022

Kaeden Corporation
3400 Chrisfield Drive
Cleveland, OH 44116

LINK
1895 Dudley Street
Lakewood, CO 80215

Modern Curriculum Press
13900 Prospect Road
Cleveland, OH 44136

Peguis Publishers Ltd.
520 Hargrauest
Winnipeg, MB, R3A OX8
Canada

Puffin Books
625 Madison Avenue
New York, NY 10022

Rigby
PO Box 797
Crystal Lake, IL 60039
1-800-822-8661

Scholastic, Inc.
730 Broadway
New York, NY 10003

School Zone Publishing
PO Box 692
Grand Haven, MI 49417

Simon & Schuster
Rockefeller Center
1230 Avenue of the Americas
New York, NY 10020
1-800-929-8765

Troll Associates
100 Corporate Drive
Mahwah, NJ 07430

The Wright Group
19201 120th Avenue NE
Bothell, WA 98011
1-800-523-2371

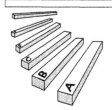

References

Adams, M. J. 1990. *Beginning to read: Thinking and learning about print*. Cambridge, MA: MIT Press.

Butler, A. 1994. *Focus on spelling*. Crystal Lake, IL: Rigby. Video. VHS. Running Time: 35 minutes.

Chall, J. S. 1983. *The great debate*. Updated ed. New York: McGraw-Hill.

Clay, M. 1985. *The early detection of reading difficulties*. 3d ed. Portsmouth, NH: Heinemann Educational Books.

———. 1991. *Becoming literate: The construction of inner control*. Portsmouth, NH: Heinemann Educational Books.

———. 1993. *Reading recovery: A guidebook for teachers in training*. Portsmouth, NH: Heinemann Educational Books.

DeFord, D., Lyons, C., and Pinnell, G. 1991. *Bridges to literacy: Learning from reading recovery*. Portsmouth, NH: Heinemann Educational Books.

Goodman, K. 1994. Presentation at the Colorado Council of the International Reading Association. 4 February 1994.

Graves, D. 1994. *A fresh look at writing*. Portsmouth, NH: Heinemann Educational Books.

Holdaway, D. 1979. *The foundations of literacy*. Gosford, N.S.W.: Ashton Scholastic.

Lawson, M., et al. 1993. *CLIP manual*. Tempe, AZ: Tempe School District #3.

Lyons, C., Pinnell, G., and DeFord, D. 1993. *Partners in learning: Teachers and children in Reading Recovery*. New York: Teachers College Press.

Pinnell, G., in Allen and Mason. 1989. *Risk makers, risk takers, risk breakers*. Portsmouth, NH: Heinemann Educational Books.

Routman, R. 1991. *Invitations*. Portsmouth, NH: Heinemann Educational Books.

———. 1988. *Transitions*. Portsmouth, NH: Heinemann Educational Books.

Sitton, R. 1990. Increasing student spelling achievement. Handout given at Colorado Council of the International Reading Association. 3 February 1990.

Smith, F. 1983. *Essays into literacy*. Concord, Ontario: Irwin.

———. 1988. *Understanding reading*. 4th ed. Hillsdale, NJ: Laurence Erlbaum.

Stanovich, K. 1994. "Romance and reality." *The Reading Teacher* 47: 28-291.

Traill, L. 1994. *Learning running records*. Crystal Lake, IL: Rigby. Video. VHS. Running Time: 21:30 minutes.

———. 1994. *Using running records*. Crystal Lake, IL: Rigby. Video. VHS. Running Time: 27 minutes.

———. 1994. *Reading in the junior classes*. Wellington, New Zealand: Learning Media.

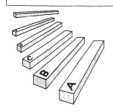

Suggestions for Further Reading

Books

Buchanan, E. *Spelling for Whole Language Classrooms*. Winnipeg, Manitoba: Whole Language Consultants, 1989. Describes developmental stages of spelling and presents strategies and activities for each stage. Includes excellent section on evaluating spelling errors.

Clay, M. *An Observation Survey of Early Literacy Achievement*. Portsmouth, NH: Heinemann Educational Books, 1993. Describes diagnostic instruments that can be used when observing young children's literacy development.

Eggleton, J. *Whole Language Evaluation*. Hong Kong: Applecross, 1990. Presents practical record-keeping systems teachers may adapt to their classroom situations.

Fry, E. *The New Reading Teacher's Book of Lists*. Englewood Cliffs, NJ: Prentice-Hall, 1985. Includes over 100 lists of words; categories range from phonetic generalizations to fun words like palindromes and homonyms.

Gentry, R. *Spel Is a Four Letter Word*. Portsmouth, NH: Heinemann Educational Books, 1987. Describes developmental stages of spelling in easy-to-read format; excellent resource to share with parents.

Gentry, R., and Gillet, J. *Teaching Kids to Spell*. Portsmouth, NH: Heinemann Educational Books, 1993. Offers guidelines for a school-wide spelling program in addition to word lists and teaching tips to help students in different developmental stages.

Kaye, C. *Word Works*. Covelo, CA: Yolla Bolly Press, 1985. Offers suggestions and activities that encourage children to have fun with words.

Phinney, M. *Reading with the Troubled Reader*. Portsmouth, NH: Heinemann Educational Books, 1988. Describes universal reading principles and five types of troubled readers; offers suggestions for working with each type of struggling reader.

Pratt, N., and Darcy, L. *Scribbles to Sentences*. Golden, CO: Jefferson County Public Schools, 1987. Explains the developmental stages of writing in clear and concise language; excellent resource to share with parents.

Sitton, R. *Spelling Sourcebook I*. Spokane, WA: Rebecca Sitton, 1995. Offers many spelling games and activities to increase children's awareness of words and sense of discovery.

Strouf, J. *The Literature Teacher's Book of Lists*. West Nyack, NY: Center for Applied Research in Education, 1993. Lists works of literature according to genre, theme, period, and other useful categories.

Reports

Sweet, A. "Transforming Ideas for Teaching and Learning to Read." Washington, D.C.: U. S. Government Printing Office, 1993. Discusses ten ideas about learning and teaching reading that emerged from research conducted by the U.S. Department of Education.

————. "Becoming a Nation of Readers: The Report of the Commission on Reading." Los Angeles: The Economy Company, 1985. Defines reading and emerging literacy and presents the seventeen recommendations of the commission.

Articles

Cunningham, P., and Cunningham, J. "Making Words: Enhancing the Invented Spelling-Decoding Connection." *The Reading Teacher* 46 (October 1992): 106-13.

Griffith, P., and Olson, M. "Phonemic Awareness Helps Beginning Readers Break the Code." *The Reading Teacher* 45 (March 1992): 516-23.

Gunning, T. "Word Building: A Strategic Approach to the Teaching of Phonics." *The Reading Teacher* 48 (March 1995): 484-88.

Stahl, S. "Saying the 'P' Word: Nine Guidelines for Exemplary Phonics Instruction." *The Reading Teacher* 45 (April 1992): 618-25.

Yopp, H. "Developing Phonemic Awareness in Young Children." *The Reading Teacher* 45 (May 1992): 696-703.

———. "A Test for Assessing Phonemic Awareness in Young Children." *The Reading Teacher* 49 (September 1995): 20-29.

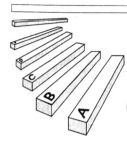

Index

Children's Literature Cited

Title	Publisher	Page Location
Aaron and Gayla's Alphabet	Black Butterfly Children's Books	5
All Join In	Rigby	73
All of Me	Rigby	92, 99
Along Comes Jake	Wright Group	71, 78, 84, 101, 109
Alphabears	Henry Holt	5
Alphabet Bandits	Troll	5, 8
Anansi and the Moss-Covered Rock	Scholastic	60
Animals at the Zoo	Troll	45, 55, 72, 74, 79, 83, 89, 110, 114
Anna Banana and Me	Houghton Mifflin	35, 39
Annie and the Wild Animals	Houghton Mifflin	32
Ant and the Dove, The	Rigby	35
Ants Love Picnics Too	Rigby	47, 90, 103
Apple Tree! Apple Tree!	Children's Press	47
Are You a Ladybug?	Wright Group	11, 14
Are You My Mother?	Random House	91, 114
Ashanti to Zulu: African Traditions	Dial Books	6, 63
Ask Mr. Bear	Collier Books	32, 35
At the Carnival	DLM	74, 80, 89, 102, 109
At the Zoo	DLM	55, 73, 85, 88, 98, 110
Baby Gets Dressed	Wright Group	101, 115
Baby Panda at the Fair	DLM	51, 60, 74, 80, 85, 91, 96

Title	Publisher	Page Location
Baby's Birthday	Rigby	74, 83, 96
Baby's Dinner	Rigby	11, 31, 37
Bath for a Beagle, A	Troll	52, 84, 85, 93
Bean Bag That Mom Made, The	Rigby	13
Bear's Busy Year	Troll	37, 101
Bears	Harper & Row	14
Bears in the Night	Random House	47
Beautiful Breezy Blue and White Day	DLM	60, 90, 102
Bee, The	Wright Group	86, 94, 95
Berenstain's B Book	Random House	5
Bicycle, The	Wright Group	10, 20, 72, 82, 94
Big and Little	Wright Group	74, 83, 89
Big Brown Teddy Bear, The	DLM	74, 89, 105, 107
Big Enormous Turnip, The	LINK	18, 64, 78, 84, 96,
Big Hill, The	Wright Group	10, 106
Birthday Buddies	Troll	27, 90, 97
Birthday Cake, The	Rigby	94, 111
Blue Ribbon Puppies, The	Harper & Row	48
Blue Sea	Greenwillow Books	74, 75, 89, 111
Boney-Legs	Scholastic	64
Bread	Wright Group	83, 98, 100, 102
Breakfast in Bed	Rigby	27
Bringing the Rain to Kapiti Plain	Dial Books	63
Brown Bear, Brown Bear, What Do You See?	Holt, Rinehart & Winston	59, 79, 90, 99, 107, 110, 111, 114
Bubble Gum in the Sky	Troll	20, 24, 75, 80, 83
Buffy	Rigby	77

Title	Publisher	Page Location
Bulldozer, The	Rigby	52
Bunny Hop, The	Scholastic	47
Busy Beavers	Scholastic	27
Butterflies and Moths	National Education	36, 64
Buzzing Flies	Wright Group	41, 73, 102
Caps for Sale	Harper & Row	18, 20, 64, 111
Caps, Hats, Socks and Mittens	Scholastic	11
Carla's New Friends	DLM	35, 113
Carrot Seed, The	Scholastic	52, 76, 93, 104, 109, 111
Caterpillar Diary	Rigby	64
Cement Tent, The	Troll	11, 17, 103
Chatty Chipmunk's Nutty Day	Troll	41
Chew Chew Chew	Rigby	11, 41, 43
Chicka-Chicka Boom Boom	Scholastic	5
Chicken Little	Houghton Mifflin	28
Chicken Little	Mimosa	28
Chicken Salad Soup	Modern Curriculum Press	51, 52
Chicken Soup with Rice	Scholastic	56, 60, 95, 104, 109, 113
Chocolate Cake, The	Wright Group	97, 112, 115
Circus, The	Rigby	101
City Seen from A to Z	Greenwillow Books	5
Claude the Dog	Clarion Books	32
Clean House for Mole and Mouse, A	Scholastic	47
Clown, The	Kaeden Corporation	95, 96, 110
Come and Have Fun	Harper & Row	74, 78, 84, 108
Come for a Swim	Wright Group	63, 78, 108

Title	Publisher	Page Location
Come On Up!	Troll	23, 24, 39, 77, 85, 101, 103, 104
Come with Me	Wright Group	77, 91, 109
Cookie's Week	Scholastic	21, 80, 102, 105, 112, 116
Copy-Cat	Wright Group	82, 87, 104, 109
Corduroy	Scholastic	64
Country Mouse and City Mouse	Regensteiner Publishing	37, 56, 58
Cowboy Alphabet	Pelican Publishing	6
Crocodile Beat	Rigby	5, 15, 59
Dan, the Flying Man	Wright Group	10, 13, 77, 86, 91, 96, 109
Danger	Wright Group	73, 81, 90, 94, 95, 102
Debra's Dog	Rigby	5, 8
Dining with Prunella	Small Package	6
Dinner!	Wright Group	10, 104
Dinosaur Alphabet Book	Troll	6
Dinosaur Ball, The	DLM	60, 76, 106, 113
Dizzy Lizzy	Rigby	73, 90
Don't Wake the Baby	Rigby	74, 79
Don't You Laugh at Me	Wright Group	51, 54, 77, 79, 86, 94, 95
Doorbell Rang, The	Scholastic	76, 91, 101, 113
Down by the Bay	Crown	74, 75, 79, 81, 98, 108
Down to Town	Wright Group	47, 79, 82
Dr. Seuss's ABC	Random House	6
Dragon, The	Modern Curriculum Press	56
Dragons Are Singing Tonight, The	Scholastic	56
Dream in a Wishing Well, A	DLM	28, 44, 75, 76, 77, 101, 109, 113
Dressing Up	Rigby	94, 96, 102

Title	Publisher	Page Location
Drummer Hoff	Simon & Schuster	5, 75
Each Peach Pear Plum	Scholastic	4
Easter Bunny's Lost Egg	Troll	20, 85, 108
Eating the Alphabet: Fruits and Vegetables from A to Z	Harcourt Brace Jovanovich	5
Elephant in Trouble	Troll	72, 84, 107
Enormous Watermelon, The	Rigby	64
Excuses, Excuses	Rigby	11
Exploding Frog, The	Modern Curriculum Press	32
Farm Concert, The	Wright Group	44, 77, 106, 115
Farm, The	Rigby	101
Farmer's Alphabet, A	David R. Godine	4, 5, 8
Feet	Wright Group	14, 114
Five Little Kittens	Troll	76, 82, 84, 96, 98, 113
Five Little Monkeys Jumping on the Bed	Clarion Books	63, 80, 88, 94, 98, 113, 115
Fix-It	E. P. Dutton	111
Fizz and Splutter	Wright Group	86, 90, 93, 94, 101, 105, 107, 111
Fly, Fly Witchy	Rigby	59
Fly Went By, A	Random House	24, 60
Flying	DLM	79, 86, 95, 104
Flying High	DLM	78, 88, 92
Four Fur Feet	Doubleday	5
Fox in Socks	Random House	6
Freddie the Frog	Troll	71, 76, 95, 98, 104, 115
Frederick	Alfred A. Knopf	21
Freight Train	Scholastic	55
Friendly Snowman	Troll	90, 92, 106, 109

Title	Publisher	Page Location
Frog and Toad Are Friends	Harper & Row	33
Frog and Toad Together	Harper & Row	63
Fruit Salad	Rigby	100
Getting Ready for the Ball	Rigby	84, 101
Ghost, The	Wright Group	71, 99, 101
Go, Go, Go	Wright Group	85, 114
Going Fishing	Rigby	11
Going to School	Wright Group	81, 92, 103, 106
Good for You	Wright Group	14, 32, 35, 81, 82, 110
Good Night, Owl	Houghton Mifflin	39, 64
Goodbye, Lucy	Wright Group	81, 83, 100, 110, 115
Goodnight Moon	Harper & Row	72, 82, 91
Grandpa Snored	Rigby	32, 51
Greedy Cat	School Publications	55
Greedy Gray Octopus, The	Rigby	31, 37, 55
Green Bananas	Rigby	28
Green Eyes	Rigby	75, 90, 93
Grouchy Ladybug, The	Harper & Row	80, 94, 98, 105, 114
Grumpy Elephant	Wright Group	55, 58, 63, 71, 86,
Gum on the Drum, The	School Zone	10, 21, 24
Happy Birthday	Rigby	77, 81, 83, 112
Harold and the Purple Crayon	Scholastic	91
Harry and the Terrible Whatzit	Scholastic	39
Haunted House, The	Wright Group	72, 74, 89
Have You Seen?	Rigby	94, 116
Have You Seen Birds?	Scholastic	45, 51, 60

Title	Publisher	Page Location
Hearing Things	Children's Press	56
Hello	Wright Group	98, 103
Here Are My Hands	Henry Holt	59, 73, 81, 84, 87, 92
Here Comes Winter	Troll	28, 81, 83, 87, 107
Hi, All You Rabbits	Parents' Magazine Press	45
Hi-De-Hi	Scott Foresman	45
Home for a Puppy	Troll	82, 85, 96
Horace	Wright Group	71, 77, 93, 94, 97, 100, 109
House Is a House for Me, A	Scholastic	17
Houses	Wright Group	72, 86, 87, 102, 111
How Much Is a Million?	Scholastic	91
How Spider Saved Easter	Scholastic	56
Hug Is Warm, A	Wright Group	73, 105
Huggles' Breakfast	Wright Group	71, 115
Huggles Can Juggle	Wright Group	20, 72
Huggles Goes Away	Wright Group	100
Hungry Horse	Rigby	41, 72
Hurry Hurry	Rigby	28
I Am a Bookworm	Wright Group	55, 104
I Am Frightened	Wright Group	72, 81, 94
I Can Fly	Wright Group	79, 104, 115
I Can Jump	Wright Group	76, 77
I Can Spell Dinosaur	DLM	11, 76, 77, 85
I Can Squeak	Heinemann	44, 46
I Hear	Greenwillow Books	44
I Know an Old Lady	Rand McNally	72, 79, 83, 88, 94, 99, 108

Title	Publisher	Page Location
I Like	Rigby	88
I Like the Rain	Wright Group	14
I Like What I Am	Modern Curriculum Press	17
I Love Ladybugs	DLM	76, 85, 90, 92, 111, 112
I Love My Family	Wright Group	85, 90, 92, 112
I Love You, Good Night	Simon & Schuster	5, 89, 110
I Saw a Dinosaur	Rigby	98
I Spy	Rigby	27, 86, 116
I Want a Pet	School Zone	10
I Want Ice Cream	Wright Group	114
I Was Walking Down the Road	Scholastic	32, 59, 77, 79, 96, 98, 101
I Wish I Were a Butterfly	Harcourt Brace	37
I'm Bigger Than You	Wright Group	24, 75, 86, 93, 100, 110, 111
I'm Tyrannosaurus	G. P. Putnam's Sons	5, 60
Ice Cream	Wright Group	88, 106
Icky Bug Alphabet Book, The	Charlesbridge	6, 8, 56
If I Were a Fish	DLM	37, 75, 86, 106
If You Give a Moose a Muffin	Harper & Row	112
If You Give a Mouse a Cookie	Harper & Row	10, 112
If You Meet a Dragon	Wright Group	85
In My Bed	Rigby	81, 92, 97, 102
In My Room	Rigby	76, 87, 88, 92, 97
In the Mirror	Wright Group	92, 99
Inside, Outside, Upside Down	Random House	20
Is Your Mama a Llama?	Scholastic	18, 63
It Could Still Be a Bird	Children's Press	37, 44, 45, 51

Title	Publisher	Page Location
It Could Still Be a Fish	Children's Press	37, 51
It Looked Like Spilt Milk	Harper & Row	60, 89, 90, 100
It's a Good Thing There Are Insects	Children's Press	56
Itchy Itchy Chicken Pox	Scholastic	41
Jack and the Beanstalk	Rigby	41
Jack-in-the-Box	Rigby	10, 75, 86, 87, 111
Jack-o-lantern	Wright Group	17
Jacket I Wear in the Snow, The	Scholastic	32
Jigaree, The	Wright Group	59, 62, 76, 80, 87, 99, 102
Jillian Jiggs	Scholastic	33
Jolly Monster, The	Troll	27
Just for You	Golden Book	75, 81, 88, 104, 105, 110
Just Grandpa and Me	Golden Book	32
Just Like Daddy	Scholastic	78, 88
Kangaroo's Umbrella	Modern Curriculum Press	20, 56
Kangaroo, The	Modern Curriculum Press	56
Kitten Twins, The	Troll	113
Kittens	Wright Group	20, 112
Knight and the Dragon, The	G. P. Putnam's Sons	48
Ladybugs	Franklin Watts	14
Leo the Late Bloomer	Windmill Books	78, 112
Let's Get a Pet	Troll	11, 76, 100, 102, 104, 109, 110
Let's Have a Swim	Wright Group	83, 88, 95
Let's Take Care of the Earth	Creative Teaching Press	17, 18
Light in the Attic, A	Harper & Row	33
Lilly-Lolly Little Legs	Rigby	59, 77, 81, 86, 92, 110

Title	Publisher	Page Location
Little Brother	Wright Group	31, 83, 90, 112
Little Danny Dinosaur	Troll	24, 35, 74, 87, 89, 93, 104, 105, 112, 114
Little Pig	Wright Group	82, 85, 92, 97, 115
Little Red Hen, The	Clarion Books	64
Long, Long Tail	Wright Group	14, 94
Look for Me	Wright Group	80, 85, 90, 93, 97, 99
Looking for Halloween	Kaeden	76, 80
Lost	Wright Group	78, 79, 92, 105
Mag the Magnificent	Clarion Books	56
Major Jump	Wright Group	72, 113
Maligned Mosquito, The	DLM	73, 79, 80, 88, 97, 104, 108
Marching Band, The	Kaeden	31, 34, 55, 76, 96
Margie and Me	Four Winds Press	18
Marvelous Me	Rigby	95
Mike's New Bike	Troll	17
Miss Nelson Is Missing	Houghton Mifflin	98, 116
Mitten, The	Putnam Pub Group	47
Mixed-Up Chameleon, The	Harper & Row	48, 89, 109
Mom Can Fix Anything	Creative Teaching Press	17
Mom's Haircut	Rigby	112
Mongon	DLM	75, 79, 88, 98, 102, 115
Monkey Bridge, The	Wright Group	96, 106, 113
Monster Meals	Rigby	82, 86
Monster Sandwich, A	Wright Group	87, 94, 96, 100
Monster Under My Bed, The	Troll	27, 35, 43, 98, 101, 104, 107
Monsters' Party, The	Wright Group	76, 77, 107, 114

Title	Publisher	Page Location
Mooncake	Scholastic	37
More and More Clowns	DLM	55, 73, 78, 91, 94, 95, 111
More Bugs in Boxes	Simon & Schuster	5
Mother, Mother, I Want Another	Crown	72, 91, 105, 115, 116
Mouse	Wright Group	20, 112
Mr. Brown Can Moo!	Random House	48
Mr. Grump	Wright Group	63, 108
Mrs. Sato's Hens	Scott Foresman	20, 21
Mrs. Wishy Washy	Wright Group	11, 37, 63, 72, 87, 94, 98, 106
Mud Pies	Troll	73, 87, 89, 91, 100, 112
Muffy and Fluffy	Troll	71, 98, 102
Munching Mark	Rigby	41, 55
My Home	Wright Group	17, 20, 84, 85, 87, 88, 92, 97
My Puppy	Wright Group	26, 30, 92, 96, 114
My Wonderful Aunt, Story 2	Wright Group	18
Napping House, The	Harcourt Brace Jovanovich	60
New Baby Calf, The	Scholastic	63
Night-Train, The	Wright Group	71, 102
Night-Time	Wright Group	86, 87
No, No	Wright Group	10, 13, 24, 71, 72, 77, 91, 93, 100
No, No Joan	School Book Fairs	93, 103, 105
Noises	Rigby	103
Noisy Neighbors	Troll	78, 91, 93, 103, 108
Noisy Nora	Scholastic	24
Now I Know Animals at Night	Troll	39
Now I Know Bears	Troll	51, 52

Title	Publisher	Page Location
Now I Know Birds	Troll	52
Now I Know Changing Seasons	Troll	32, 37
Now I Know Clouds	Troll	32
Now I Know Horses	Troll	51
Now I Know Stars	Troll	52
Now I Know Trees	Troll	14, 47
Obadiah	Wright Group	12, 84, 87, 88, 105
Oh, Jump in a Sack	Wright Group	44, 74, 78, 86, 94, 95, 106, 109
Old Black Fly	Scholastic	4
Old Steam Train, The	Rigby	109
On a Chair	Wright Group	89, 90, 95, 102, 108
On a Cold, Cold Day	Rigby	55
On Monday When It Rained	Houghton Mifflin	17, 64, 112
On the Farm	Rigby	82
One Bright Monday Morning	Silver Burdett & Ginn	59
One Light, One Sun	Crown	80, 95
One, One Is the Sun	Wright Group	113
Our Baby	Rigby	84
Our Dog Sam	Rigby	89, 95, 103
Our Granny	Wright Group	17, 18, 99, 107
Our Street	Wright Group	85, 87, 103
Over in the Meadow	Scholastic	12, 15, 89, 96, 98, 113, 115
Owl Moon	Scholastic	15
Ox-Cart Man	Scholastic	64
Painting	Wright Group	72, 101
Pancakes for Supper	Rigby	52, 78, 96, 104

Title	Publisher	Page Location
Panda, The	Modern Curriculum Press	51
Papa, Please Get the Moon for Me	Picture Book Studio	83, 100, 105
Party, The	Wright Group	71
Peanut Butter and Jelly	E. P. Dutton	87, 101
Penguins Come to Dinner, The	DLM	73, 75, 78, 86, 101, 102, 108
Pet Parade, The	Rigby	76, 86
Pets	Rigby	47
Pickle Things	Parents Magazine Press	44
Planting a Rainbow	Harcourt Brace Jovanovich	31, 111
Playground Fun	Troll	80, 81, 102
Plop!	Wright Group	76, 83, 99
Polar Bear, Polar Bear, What Do You Hear?	Henry Holt	59, 79, 84, 107, 110, 114
Potluck	Orchard Books	5, 6
Praying Mantis, The	Modern Curriculum Press	32
Pumpkin, Pumpkin	Scholastic	32, 52
Pumpkin, The	Wright Group	55, 63, 71, 83, 106, 112
Puppet Show	Troll	90, 106
Q Is for Duck	Clarion Books	44, 108
Quick as a Cricket	Child's Play (International)	6
Race, The	Wright Group	82, 93, 107, 109
Red Is Best	Firefly Books	74, 92, 98, 110, 111
Red Rose, The	Wright Group	74, 85, 97, 99, 106
Rhinoceros? Preposterous!, A	DLM	52, 95, 114, 115
Rice	Modern Curriculum Press	55, 56
Rooster and the Weather Vane, The	Troll	17, 24, 39
Rooster's Off to See the World	Picture Book Studio	63

Title	Publisher	Page Location
Rosie's Walk	Collier Books	10, 73, 112
Round and Round	Wright Group	72, 97
Rub-a-Dub Suds	Troll	96
Rum-tum-tum	Wright Group	73
Sam the Scarecrow	Troll	90, 98, 105
Sandcake	Parents Magazine Press	114
Scarecrow, The	Rigby	87, 98
"Scat!" Said the Cat	Wright Group	39, 97, 114, 115
Scruffy Messed It Up	Rigby	75, 106
Scrumptious Sundae, A	Rigby	100, 115
Secret Birthday Message, The	Harper & Row	47, 112
See You Later, Alligator	Price Stern Sloan	6, 99
Seed Song, The	Creative Teaching Press	14
Seed, The	Wright Group	63, 75, 78, 83, 102
Sharing	Rigby	80, 91, 95, 109
Shark in a Sack	Wright Group	76, 96, 110
Sheep in a Jeep	Houghton Mifflin	14, 16
Shoo!	Wright Group	37, 74, 75, 106
Should You Ever?	Peguis	71, 80, 92, 99, 109
Silly Old Possum	Wright Group	41, 112
Six Sleepy Sheep	Puffin Books	5
Skating on Thin Ice	Troll	24, 27, 89, 100
Sleeping Out	Wright Group	82, 99, 101, 103, 107
Snail, The	Modern Curriculum Press	18
Snap!	Wright Group	100
Snoopy's Book of Opposites	Golden Book	5, 113

Title	Publisher	Page Location
Snowflakes	Kaeden	92, 95
Spider in the Shower, The	Rigby	48
Spider, Spider	Wright Group	24, 26, 31, 37, 51, 77, 91, 93
Splosh!	Wright Group	114, 115
Sticky Stanley	Troll	84, 99, 104
Stone Soup	Checkerboard Press	56
Stop!	Wright Group	31, 75, 94, 106
Storm, The	Wright Group	78
Summer Camp	Rigby	37, 56
Sunrise	Rigby	81, 97, 103, 104, 115
Surprise Cake	Rigby	79
Surprise Party, The	Aladdin Books	27
Surprise, The	Rigby	59, 93, 109
Tadpole Diary	Rigby	20
Teeny Tiny	Houghton Mifflin	18, 82, 100, 107
Teeny Tiny Tina	Rigby	26, 71, 72, 86
Teeny Tiny Woman	Clarion Books	82, 100, 107
Ten Little Men	Rigby	113
Ten Pennies for Candy	Holt, Rinehart & Winston	28
There Was an Old Lady	Child's Play (International)	72, 79, 88, 94, 96, 99, 102, 105, 108
There's a Dragon in My Wagon	Modern Curriculum Press	79, 88, 92, 102
There's a Nightmare in My Closet	Dial Books	27, 64, 112
There's an Alligator Under My Bed	Dial Books	27
There's Something in My Attic	Dial Books	27
Things That Go—A Traveling Alphabet	Byron Press Visual	6
This Is the Bear	Harper & Row	39

Title	Publisher	Page Location
Three Billy Goats Gruff	Regensteiner	24, 35
Three Billy Goats Gruff	Scholastic	75, 89, 98, 101, 108, 116
Three Dogs at My Door	DLM	84, 86, 95, 105, 107
Three Little Ducks	Wright Group	31, 44, 63
Three Little Kittens	Random House	48
Timmy	Rigby	105
To New York	Wright Group	115
To Town	Wright Group	51, 71, 74, 82, 87, 103, 106, 109, 111
Tommy's Tummy Ache	Rigby	13, 41, 56, 72
Too Big for Me	Wright Group	74, 77, 81, 84, 91, 97, 103, 107
Too Many Clothes	Rigby	31, 32, 101
Tooth Fairy, The	Troll	35
Toybox, A	Rigby	71
Tree House, The	Wright Group	104, 106
Tree Stump, The	Scott, Foresman	47
Tree, The	Modern Curriculum Press	14
Turtle Tale	Scholastic	35
Two Little Dogs	Wright Group	71, 97, 102
Umbrella Parade	Troll	74, 78, 82, 84, 109, 111
Uncle Buncle's House	Wright Group	73, 102, 113
Unicorn Alphabet	Dial Books	5, 8
Up in a Tree	Wright Group	78, 99, 104, 107, 114
Valentine's Day Grump	Troll	39
Very Busy Spider, The	Philomel Books	73, 78, 84, 99, 104, 105, 114, 115
Very Hungry Caterpillar, The	Philomel Books	111, 112, 113
Very Quiet Cricket, The	Philomel Books	60, 73, 83, 89, 103, 105

Title	Publisher	Page Location
Visitors	Rigby	27
Wake Up, Mom	Wright Group	81, 101, 105
Watch Out!	Rigby	106
Watch Your Step, Mr. Rabbit	Random House	76, 85, 90, 95, 106
Wedding, The	Rigby	47
What a Dog!	Troll	51, 52, 97, 98, 102
What a Mess!	Wright Group	80, 86, 97, 107, 110, 115
What Are You?	Rigby	71, 114
What Can Fly?	Rigby	20
What Can You Do?	Peguis	76, 96
What Can You Hear?	Peguis	59, 76
What Can You See?	Peguis	76, 85, 99
What Did Kim Catch?	Rigby	77
What Did You Put in Your Pocket?	Scott Foresman	27
What Do You Do?	Peguis	79, 93, 110
What Do You Have?	Peguis	79, 83, 93, 110
What Do You Hear?	Peguis	84
What Goes in the Bathtub?	Rigby	93
What Has Spots?	Rigby	83, 103
What Is a Huggles?	Wright Group	87, 93
What Is It?	Peguis	55
What Is This?	Peguis	87, 103
What Will the Weather Be Like Today?	Scholastic	31, 32, 35, 39
What Would You Like?	Wright Group	88, 109, 114
What's for Lunch?	Wright Group	81, 93, 97, 107
What's Going On?	Creative Teaching Press	14

Title	Publisher	Page Location
What's In My Pocket?	Creative Teaching Press	44
Wheels	Rigby	47, 95
Wheels on the Bus	Crown	47, 50, 71, 73, 82, 97, 104
When I Play	Rigby	107
When I Was Sick	Rigby	51, 105, 107
When Itchy Witchy Sneezes	Wright Group	41, 73, 75, 99
When Lana Was Absent	Rigby	24
Where Are They Going?	Wright Group	73, 87, 90, 103, 108, 114
Where Are You Going, Aja Rose?	Wright Group	82, 88, 108
Where Do You Live?	Peguis	79, 89, 108, 110, 114
Where Is My Shoe?	Holt, Rinehart & Winston	5, 27
Where Is Nancy?	Rigby	99
Where the Sidewalk Ends	Harper & Row	8
Where the Wild Things Are	Harper & Row	64, 66, 103, 108
Where's That Duck?	Children's Press	44
Who Cried for Pie?	Troll	63, 108, 112, 114
Who Likes Ice Cream?	Rigby	78
Who Lives Here?	Wright Group	108, 113
Who Will Be My Mother?	Wright Group	72, 74, 77, 91, 103, 106, 110, 115
Who's Going to Lick the Bowl?	Wright Group	72, 115
Who's Hiding?	Creative Teaching Press	51
Who's in the Shed?	Rigby	37, 39, 43
Whose Mouse Are You?	Scholastic	39, 43, 52, 108, 110, 113
Why Can't I Fly?	Scholastic	21, 76, 80, 116
Why Do Polar Bears Like the Arctic?	Rigby	35, 39, 51
Wildlife ABC, The	Half Moon Books	6

Title	Publisher	Page Location
Wilfred the Lion	G. P. Putnam's Sons	48
Wind Blows Strong, The	Wright Group	37, 90
Wishy Washy Day	Wright Group	11, 63
Yes Ma'am	Wright Group	28
Yuk Soup	Wright Group	82, 86, 100
Yummers!	Houghton Mifflin	56
Yummy, Yummy	Troll	17
Z Was Zapped, The	Houghton Mifflin	6
Zoo, A	Rigby	71

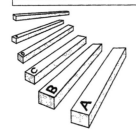

About the Author

Karen has spent most of her professional career teaching reading, either as a primary grade classroom teacher, or as a reading specialist. She received her Bachelor of Science degree from St. John College of Cleveland and her Master of Arts in reading from the University of Colorado. She has worked extensively in the area of early intervention, and presently trains teachers to deliver one-on-one instruction based on Marie Clay's Reading Recovery model. Karen particularly enjoys presenting at state reading conferences, and has had articles and poetry published in various professional journals. She lives in Littleton, Colorado with her husband. They, and their three grown children, continue to enjoy the beauty of the Rocky Mountains.

www.ingramcontent.com/pod-product-compliance
Ingram Content Group UK Ltd.
Pitfield, Milton Keynes, MK11 3LW, UK
UKHW050147280225
455689UK00007B/92